To Alistair,

Lots of Lov

from

Kirsty xxx

HARRY WAS A C[illegible] HAT

First published in 2009 by

WOODFIELD PUBLISHING LTD
Bognor Regis ~ West Sussex ~ England ~ PO21 5EL
www.woodfieldpublishing.com

ISBN 1-84683-081-8

Harry Was a Crap Hat

A Soldier's Story

BRIAN CLACY

Woodfield

Woodfield Publishing Ltd

Woodfield House ~ Babsham Lane ~ Bognor Regis ~ West Sussex ~ PO21 5EL
telephone 01243 821234 ~ **e-mail** enquiries@woodfieldpublishing.co.uk

Interesting and informative books on a variety of subjects

For full details of all our published titles, visit our website at
www.woodfieldpublishing.co.uk

To all soldiers of the British Army
Past, Present and Future

~ CONTENTS ~

Acknowledgements

I would like to thank the following people. They have all helped, criticised, encouraged and generally annoyed me at various stages.

Dave Burr, my neighbour. I am honoured that this is only the second book that he has ever read in his life, the first being *Adrian Mole aged 13¾*. I wish I'd had a father like Dave when I was a boy.

My close friend Ritchie John, whose help has been invaluable. His parts in the book and my life have given me so many laughs. He is currently a Detective Chief Inspector with Hampshire Constabulary in Portsmouth.

SSgt Steve Cowie, Royal Logistic Corps and Ex Royal Corps of Transport – thanks for refreshing my memory.

Audrey Middlemass, my porridge-gobbling friend, who laughed at all my early drafts.

Particular thanks must go to my very good friend Adam 'three in a night' Broom who, along with my son Matthew Fairclough, has gone through every chapter of this book with me as I have created it.

You have all hindered me beyond belief.

The biggest thanks must go to the person who originally thought up the idea of this book and believed that I could write it – my beautiful wife Nicky.

Introduction

"ARE YOU AIRBORNE OR WHAT?" screamed Corporal Wright in my face. I was supposed to shout back "ALL THE WAY CORPORAL!" but I felt like asking if we could talk about our differences over a nice cup of tea.

Airborne Forces of the British Army are the toughest, most motivated and fearless troops you will find anywhere in the world. Paras call all soldiers serving outside the Airborne Forces 'Crap Hats' or 'Hats' – a derogatory term for the majority of the Army, who all wear dark blue berets whereas the Paras wear a maroon one. Along with the green berets of the Royal Marines and the sand-coloured berets of the SAS, they are the hardest things in the world to win.

I didn't want to be a Crap Hat, I wanted to be a member of 63 Parachute Squadron Royal Corps of Transport – the transport support element of 5 Airborne Brigade.

The reality of what I was trying to do was now hitting me full in the face, much the same as Corporal Wright was doing with his fists as he called me a "crap hat wanker!"

I was on the 'Beat Up' – a pre-selection assessment to see if you were fit and tough enough to go through P Company. (Soldiers from any branch of the military have to go through, complete and pass the torture of P Company to qualify as an Army Paratrooper.)

It was the late summer of 1975 and I had just passed out of training at the Junior Leaders Regiment Royal Corps of Transport. Junior Leaders Regiments were Training Depots of the British Army for soldiers aged between 16 and 17 ½ years of age, where they were trained as future potential Non Commissioned Officers of the British Army.

When I arrived at Aldershot for the 'Beat Up' I thought I was at the peak of physical and mental fitness.

I wasn't – in both cases.

Maybe if I had been more mature, both physically and mentally, I might have made the grade. Having said that, Geordie, who came from the Junior Leaders Regiment with me, seemed to revel in the whole thing. If there was a fight in the accommodation block (Paras fight with each other if there aren't any Crap Hats to clobber) he would be in there shouting "Go on man! Fill him in!" and hoping the whole thing would escalate so he could join in and start bashing someone.

I didn't have it in me to carry on, so I quit.

And from that day on, Harry was a Crap Hat!

1. Ghosts Don't Exist

The Clacy family moved to 43 Mill Lane in Broomfield near Chelmsford in Essex so my father, who was a Civilian Prison Officer, could be nearer his place of work. My father, John Alfred Clacy, tried several jobs after leaving the army. His first was as a messenger for Barclays Bank in Colchester. In the 1960s, banks employed men to run minor errands; he didn't do this for long before he joined the Police Force.

On duty one night in the Oxfordshire Police Force, whilst still on probation, he noticed a gunman with a sawn-off shotgun outside a Post Office in a country village. Police officers today would contact their superiors, either on the radio or by mobile phone, but alas my father didn't have these luxuries. There wasn't even a public telephone nearby, so he decided to hide in a ditch behind a hedge and observe these blaggers until daylight, as they were likely to make their move when the Post Office opened.

As dawn arrived over the horizon it became clear that the nearest 'armed robber' was, in fact, an old tree stump and the 'shotgun' was a broken branch. He walked back to the Police Station with his patiently acquired case of hypothermia and embarrassment safely tucked under his arm.

Dixon of Dock Green he wasn't.

After 22 years in the army my father left, after reaching the rank of Warrant Officer Class 2 in the Military Provost Staff Corps (Military Prison Officers). He obviously decided to go back to what he knew best after his failed attempt at impersonating Jack Reagan and joined the Civilian Prison Service. After completing his training he was posted to HMP Chelmsford.

On his first day he was introduced to the Governor of the prison on an official interview in the admin block. My father marched into the office in his bulled boots and heavily starched shirt, banged his feet together as he halted in front of the Governor's desk, saluted him and shouted, in a good military fashion, "GOOD MORNING, SAH!"

You will now have an image of Mr Mckay in the comedy series *Porridge.* Keep that image in your head but substitute black hair for the grey.

The Governor quietly but firmly said to him, "Mr Clacy, you are no longer in the army and I am not a commissioned officer, I am a Civil Servant. Please try to behave like a normal civilian person."

This really annoyed my father, so when the interview was concluded he shouted, "THANK YOU, SAH!" saluted the Governor, about-turned and marched out in a smart military fashion. Thereafter he made a point of saluting the governor every time they met in and out of the prison.

When my dad was temporarily posted to HMP Wormwood Scrubs in London he was ordered by the governor to wear carpet slippers whilst on night duty because he was keeping the prisoners awake as he marched up and down the landings in his old army hob-nailed ammo boots. Dad refused. He reminded the governor that they were "just bloody cons that are here to pay a debt to society and us normal civilians" but, under threat of losing his job, he relinquished and wore the slippers. He made a point, though, of carrying a baton on night duties, which he tapped against the doors of the cells as he silently marched up and down the landings. You probably won't be surprised when I tell you that my father was a bit strange and he sobbed the day he had to leave the British Army.

After dad left the army we all lived in an old 3-bedroomed house that was in desperate need of some attention by some skilled artisans. Unfortunately it only got the attention of my bad-tempered and inept but rather keen DIY father. He built an extension on the back of the house to enlarge and improve the kitchen; we lived in what looked like the results of a terrorist bomb for about two years.

Trisha, my big, frightening sister, had joined the WRAF and was defending our island as an RAF Hercules paint-sprayer at RAF Lyneham. Therefore Susan (the only good-looking and brainy one in the family) had her own bedroom and David, my brother, and I shared the other. Susan was always neat and tidy and always offended if her room was desecrated by anyone who wasn't David Cassidy. She would take the old curved Bakelite door handle (complete with spindle) to school in her satchel to prevent any 'undesirables' gaining entry into her prissy little palace.

I was one of those undesirables.

I usually got home before Susan, because she went to Rainham Grammar School and I went to Broomfield Comprehensive School for Psychopaths, which was a lot closer to home. I worked out that if I put a flat-edged screwdriver into the hole where her door handle was supposed to be, it was possible to open her bedroom door. I then set about doing my impression of a whirling dervish and I turned the room upside down, scattering clothes and ornaments all over the place. I then slammed the door shut and made good my escape. Susan returned from school after a hard day of swotting and she entered a room reminiscent of Downtown Nagasaki in 1945. My God could she scream!

My father held a court of enquiry that was attended by the whole family. I remember thinking, 'I'll bet good money that I get the blame for this' and, sure enough, I was in the frame. I protested my innocence vehemently and pointed out that I couldn't get into her room, as we all knew of Susan's habit of removing the door handle every time she left her room unguarded. This fact seemed to perplex the lynch mob until I suggested that it might have been a poltergeist. Panic spread very quickly and I decided that it might be good fun to continue with this poltergeist theme, as I had got away with it, apart from a few suspicious looks from my mother.

I would get up at 3 o'clock in the morning and take the phone off the hook and leave it swinging against the wall or pull all the curtains down in the dining room. On one particular night I took a half-filled milk bottle from the fridge and turned it upside down on the coffee table with the help of a small, thin piece of plastic. After cleaning up the small amount of spillage with a bit of tissue I retired to bed, eagerly awaiting the cries of "it's a miracle" from my gullible family.

It is a wonderful thing to be the only one in on a rather terrifying joke. I spent a lot of time thinking up more mischievous ideas. Sometimes I went a bit over the top. I remember putting a large bamboo stick on the floor between David's and my bed running behind the chest of drawers. I punctured a hole in an old tennis ball and fixed it on the end of the stick. At bedtime, when David was starting to fall asleep, I would put my hand down and lift up the bamboo stick so that it would thump the underside of his bed and he would wake up screaming his head off. As my father rushed into our room, wearing his Superman Cape, I did an Oscar winning performance of appearing as terrified as David. I didn't shit myself like him though, that would be taking acting a step too far!

"Enough is enough!" shouted my father. "I'm calling in the vicar to exorcise this bloody place."

When the vicar came to our house and carried out his ecclesiastical duties, I decided it was time to call a halt to my nocturnal terror activities.

Next door, at 45 Mill Lane, lived a retired lady called Mrs Mouser who, on hearing the screaming at all ungodly hours of the night, asked my mother if certain members of our family were clinically insane. My mother reassured her it was nothing to worry about; we just had a ghost that was possessed by the devil living in our house.

It wasn't until I was 44 years old that I felt brave enough to admit to my mother that I was the one who caused all the ghostly happenings. She calmly said: "I knew it was you, you little sod, I just couldn't prove it."

My mother died of cancer about a year after my confession and my siblings and I decided to scatter her ashes in the village of Fordham, not far from the house in Chelmsford. We all felt it was the last place Mum was really happy before divorcing our father. After our small and private ceremony we decided to visit Mill Lane and reminisce about the good old days. As we stood outside our previous home, a lady came out of Mrs Mouser's house and asked us what we were doing.

"We used to live in this house over twenty years ago," said Susan.

"Are you the Clacys?" the lady asked.

We confirmed we were and she told us she had bought the place from our mum and took us inside to have a look around. The place was refurbished to a fantastic degree and immaculately clean and tidy, nothing like the hovel when the Clacy mingers resided there. I asked about the old lady next door and she told us that Mrs Mouser still lived there and was now over 90 years old but she would be more than pleased for us to pay a visit. We called next door and, sure enough, Mrs Mouser was pleased to see us. Although very frail, she was still mentally alert and when we reminded her of the poltergeist episode she said, "Oh, such dark and terrible times! I wouldn't want to go through all that again." I then admitted to what I had done all those years ago. Mrs Mouser said: "I am over 90 years old, but if I could get you over my knee I would give you the spanking of a lifetime, young man!"

I shall always remember the day when she came rushing round to our house because of some very loud shouting and screaming. I had decided that, as I was going to join the British Army, I should get in some training on how to deal with Prisoners of War and, as David looked like a suitable but small German Storm Trooper, I would practice on him. I tied his arms behind his back and then tied his ankles to his arms. He looked like an ugly trussed-up turkey ready for the Paxo Sage and Onion. I bundled him under the stairs and informed him that there were large spiders and mice in there with him.

My God, he screamed even louder than Susan!

With hindsight I suppose I should have shoved an old sweaty sock in his mouth to keep the noise down and avoid annoying the neighbours. Still, it was a learning process.

Mrs Mouser arrived like the 7th Cavalry, demanding to know what was going on.

"Nothing," I said, with the look of a cherub.

At this point, the very uncooperative David got his feet free and kicked open the cupboard door, crying like an eight-year-old. To be fair, he actually was eight years old, but he was still making an awful lot of noise for what I felt was only a minor interrogation. I told Mrs Mouser that I had bigger and better things in store for him as my training progressed.

She took him next door for his own safety.

When he came back later I chased him round the house and out into our overgrown and sadly neglected garden where Dad, the DIY Doughnut, had left the new bathroom suite that he was going to install sometime in the next decade. I lobbed a hand grenade (half a house brick) at my escaping prisoner but instead of hitting him in the head it hit the new cast iron bath stored in the garden and shattered the 'shit by moonlight' colour enamel.

'I'll bet good money I get the blame for this!' I thought.

I did get the blame, but it wasn't for another 18 months when Wiggy DIY eventually installed the bathroom suite.

"Who the bloody hell has done this?" shouted my father, on clearing the overgrown vegetation from around the bath.

I tried to appear shocked at the damage done to the enamel.

"Crikey dad! That's dreadful! Do you think the poltergeist has come back?"

His reply was short and to the point.

"Bugger off you little sod! I know it was you. I'm not as stupid as you think I look."

That was the severest punishment my father ever administered to me as a child. He shouted and swore a lot but never raised a hand to me at any stage of my life.

It was in 1974, only a couple of years later, that I was to join The Junior Leaders Regiment Royal Corps of Transport at Norton Manor Camp in Taunton.

I couldn't wait to put all my hard work and training with David into action.

2. 'Harry' is Born

The train arrived at Taunton Railway Station mid-afternoon on 5th May 1974, packed with the choice cuts of cerebrally challenged youth of the nation. After departing St Pancras Station in London all the hard-case gobshites were boasting about how easily they were going to get through Basic Training. Two minutes after arriving at Taunton Station and meeting a British Army Sergeant for the first time a few doubts seemed to creep into their over-confident minds. We all climbed into the back of a long line of Bedford RL 3 Tonners that were to take us to Norton Manor Camp to start our induction.

Norton Manor Camp was located a few miles to the west of Taunton near the village of Norton Fitzwarren and covered an area of about 130 acres. At the entrance of the camp was the Guardroom; from here ran a straight road all the way to the Armoury, which was located at the other side of the camp. On either side of this Roman-style road were grassed areas where scores of wooden huts had been erected in World War II. These huts were used for every purpose on the camp from classrooms and offices to accommodation blocks. The camp had been host to 56 Signal Battalion of the US Army before it deployed on Operation Overlord on D-Day, 6 June 1944.

Various units of the American and British Armies occupied Norton Manor Camp after its foundation. It was taken over by the Junior Leaders Regiment Royal Army Service Corps (predecessors to the Royal Corps of Transport) in April 1961. It is currently home to 40 Commando Regiment of the Royal Marines but the old huts have long since been knocked down and replaced with brick buildings.

After a brief and bumpy journey, the vehicles pulled up outside the WRVS Club and we were cordially invited to get our fat arses inside very quickly. I waited for my name to be called and went up to a corporal sitting behind a wooden table covered in slips of paper. After confirming my name the corporal thrust one of the slips of paper towards me. It had the following information typed on it:

24316524 J/DVR CLACY BJ
DALTON TROOP
C SQUADRON

"What does J/DVR stand for?" I asked the irritated corporal, who had already answered the same question over 300 times. "Junior Driver, you fucking imbecile!"

I wasn't sure what an imbecile was but as the word 'fucking' preceded it, I was fairly sure it wasn't a compliment.

"FALL IN OUTSIDE IN YOUR RELEVANT TROOPS!" shouted a sergeant after we had all been processed.

'Fall into what?' I thought.

Outside in the afternoon sunshine I heard a voice bellowing.

"ALL THE CRETINS FOR DALTON TROOP FALL IN, IN FRONT OF ME IN THREE RANKS! COME ON! FUCKING MOVE YOURSELVES!"

The bellowing voice was coming from my new Troop Sergeant, known by everyone as Sergeant 'Rock' Reed. To this very day I can remember seeing him for the first time. He stood about 6 feet tall and had a barrel chest that I firmly believed bullets would bounce off. He looked exactly like everyone's mental image of what a British Army Drill Sergeant would look like. He was wearing Number 2 Service Dress trousers and boots that were bulled to a shine that could be seen from outer space. His Heavy Duty Jersey was starched on the shoulders and elbow cotton patches so heavily that they seemed to creak every time he moved. All this was topped off with a Service Cap and he peered at us from under the peak, making him a very impressive and fearsome sight.

We were marched in an American Army/civilian style a short distance along the road to the accommodation block that was to be home for the next 18 months. All the arrivals were to be accommodated in Spider Blocks, so called because of the pattern they made if looked at from above. I was put in to Room 6, Dalton Troop, first bed on the left as you walked into the room. Where I was sleeping will not have any immediate significance to your average civilian, so for those of you who have never served in the Armed Forces, let me give you a couple of scenarios.

Scenario 1: Sgt 'Rock' Reed has come into work with the mother of all hangovers with the intention of carrying out a full kit inspection in Room 6, Dalton Troop. I am the first tethered goat he is going to be able to vent his anger on that morning. What bleeding chance do you think I had of keeping my bed and equipment in the upright position for more than thirty seconds?

Scenario 2: Room 5 decide to carry out a midnight raid on Room 6 and pummel the crap out of the first sleeping object they come across. Again, I am the first tethered goat they are going to be able to vent their anger on. What bleeding chance do you think I had of keeping my nose blood free and my bed the right way up for more than three seconds?

Yep! No bleeding chance for both of the above.

At least 'Rock' Reed gave me an extra 27 seconds.

These blocks were reputedly used during World War Two as morgues for any American servicemen killed on exercise or in combat. Some substance was given to this theory, as at the end of each room was a fire escape with a ramp, supposedly installed so they could wheel the cadavers in and out of the morgues on wheeled stretchers. Deep joy!

We were put in our rooms and introduced to the Junior Lance Corporal who was to be in charge of us for the next 6 weeks. J/Lance Corporal 'Fozzy' Fossard was a tall, lean and friendly young lad who was about half way through his training. He was going to show us how to bull our boots, iron our uniforms, make our bed blocks and all the other mundane tasks we had to do to survive the next six weeks.

The room was a long dormitory type with beams and had an orange heavy linoleum floor that had to be waxed and polished every day until we could see our reflections in it. There were ten grey metal beds perfectly lined up on each side of the long room. Each bed-space had a metal wardrobe, bedside cabinet and tubular steel chair, all in the same grey HMS Belfast colour. There was a 6-foot trestle table near the door with a grey blanket on it that the army had designated as an 'ironing board' or, in army parlance, "Board, Ironing, Flat, 6 foot, Complete with Blanket, Type for the use of, Uniform pressing."

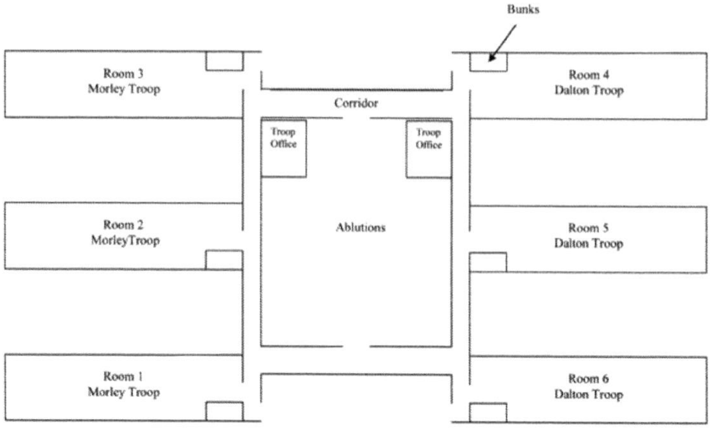

Layout of the barrack block.

There was a broad spectrum of young lads from around the country: Cockneys, Mancunians, Yorkies, Brummies and a local lad from the West Country. Some of these young lads I would grow to admire and respect and others I would grow to hate with a passion. I tried to chat to some of them but they seemed reticent to talk and appeared moody and sulky. They were probably just crapping themselves about the coming weeks.

One of these lads would unintentionally make a permanent and positive effect on my life. I was born on 7 December 1957 and christened Brian John Clacy several weeks later. I was named after a dentist my mother worked for and fell in love with when she trained as a Dental Nurse at Eastman Dental School in London. The love was unrequited, as he was a married man.

I hated the name bestowed on me because of Magic Roundabout's Brian the snail and a popular TV advert for Heinz Baked Beans at the time. One of the young lads in the advert says, in a particularly doltish voice, "I wish I could count like you Brian."

I seemed to have spent my whole life being the butt of jokes about thick kids and invertebrates. But my name was about to be changed forever and for the better.

On our first night in the room after 'lights out' there was a lot of chit-chat going on and a gobby Yorkshire lad, who had adopted a hairstyle similar to Harpo Marx, called me Harry Top Lip, referring to my slight overbite. He got a lot of laughs that night and for many weeks afterwards as the name caught on; it stuck to me like shit to a blanket. It got to the stage where I was considering leaving the army because it seemed everyone I met got a big laugh by doing their rabbit teeth impressions in front of me.

Several months into our training, one bright and beautiful morning, Taffy Burnnel and I were standing to attention outside C Squadron Office. We were waiting to have an interview with SSM 'Sluggy' Lunn to tell him exactly what he could do with his British Army because we'd had enough of it. 'Sluggy' Lunn was an exact copy of the Fat Controller in *Thomas the Tank Engine*. He had jet-black hair that was plastered to his head with Brylcreem and seemed to wobble on parade rather than march. He had a really deep and growling voice that sounded like someone was trying to throttle him. Whilst we were waiting outside his office we heard him at full volume verbally tearing the tiny testicles off some poor J/DVR. Taff turned to me and said in his soft welsh voice: "I think he is a bit busy, Harry boy. I'll come back later."

I ran after the cowardly Welsh git, who never did come back later. Neither did I.

On the afternoon of our arrival we were issued a new green cotton tracksuit, the cost of which would be deducted from our wages over the next month. Recruits in A Squadron would wear red and B Squadron blue, of exactly the same design. We wore these tracksuits the following day as we reported to the barber for haircuts. I thought I would be safe, as I had really short hair, but no, he still found enough hair to shave off to make a difference.

One short Jock lad had hair like Les McKewan out of the Bay City Rollers. After he had his haircut it was like that scene out of the cartoon Dumbo when he sneezes and his ears unfurl before everyone's eyes. I have never before or since seen a pair of ears like those. Prior to his shearing he looked quite hard but now he just looked Dopey.

Next it was off to the Quartermasters to be issued with all the military clothing and equipment that every recruit required. Inside the QM's there was a very long counter behind which lots of shelves held thousands of items of clothing and equipment. As you walked down the counter a soldier plonked down an item and shouted out what you had just been issued with.

"Vest PT White Medium Two. Red Medium One."

"Shorts PT Navy Blue Medium Two."

"Trousers Combat DPM Medium Two."

"Jacket Combat DPM Medium Two."

"Drawers Under Long Legged Green Two."

"Shirt Woollen Green Three."

"Socks Wool Green Six Pairs."

And so it went on until we had a ton of clothing and equipment all crammed into an army suitcase and a sausage shaped kitbag. I was a bit surprised when I heard, "Housewife Complete One."

'Fucking brilliant,' I thought. 'The Army are going to give us our own personal woman.' I hoped I would get a good looking one and started to wonder what sex would be like with her. Imagine my disappointment when I found out that 'she' was a small green cotton pack containing needles, cotton and spare buttons, enabling us to repair our own clothing in the field. Bummer!

Part way through our training, some of us went to Bavaria in Southern Germany on Exercise 'Snow Queen', the aim of which was to teach soldiers how to downhill and cross-country ski. The officer in charge of our party was Captain Smith, the Adjutant for the Junior Leaders Regiment RCT, who had a large handlebar moustache and talked like he had half a pound of plums and four silver spoons in his mouth.

Everyone on our course got on very well and I seemed to be very popular because I was always clowning around and making everyone laugh, including Captain Smith.

It was a fantastic two-week course and afterwards we returned to Norton Manor Camp to continue with our training. One morning, as we were marching on to the Parade Ground for morning work parade, we marched past the Adjutant, who shouted out to me, "Good morning Harry, and how are we this fine morning!"

"Fine thank you sir," I replied.

I could hear mutterings in the squad.

"Bloody Hell, that was the Adjutant. How the hell does he know who Harry is?" Several days later, on an RSM's Parade, the RSM, whilst inspecting our Troop, approached me and said, "Morning Harry! Excellent turn out!"

I loved my new name from this point onwards, as everyone left off the 'Top Lip' part. I seemed to be increasingly popular from that point onwards; people from all over the camp had heard about the comments from two of the key personnel on the camp. I don't know how or why this happened but I felt elated with my new found fame and name.

I have kept the last part of this new name secret even though so many people have asked for an explanation over the years; I still cringe at the thought of the humiliation I went through in Basic Training as an insecure 16-year-old.

I would like to thank Captain Smith and the Regimental Sergeant Major, who played such a life-changing part in my life and didn't even know it. Or did they?

Thanks also to that gobby Yorkshire Lad. You were such a cruel and arrogant bastard, who insulted me with a name that gave you a lot of laughs at my expense. Little did you know what a great favour to me that was to be…

For all of you that read this and say "that was hardly worth waiting for" I make no apologies.

If you meet me in the street or at a party and wish to call me the full name of 'Harry Top Lip' out loud, I will beat you to within an inch of your miserable fucking life. And I will only be letting you off that lightly because it doesn't bother me any more.

3. Shitting with an Audience

We'd spent 12 months being instructed in marching, weapon training, first aid, nuclear, biological and chemical warfare, fieldcraft and all the other stuff you need to know to be a soldier. All this before we got anywhere near any trucks, which were what we had joined the army to drive.

I eventually got into Senior Troop. This was the last part of our training at the Junior Leaders Regiment. It was in Senior Troop that we started the entire driver training phase, which included Basic Fault Finding on the Internal Combustion Engine.

In the Military you have to First Parade any vehicle before you take it out on a detail. This involves checking the oil, petrol, tyre pressures, lights, etc. I enjoyed this to a degree, as I felt like a pilot checking out his Spitfire before setting out to fight the Hun in the sun during the Battle of Britain. However, all these checks were done by me in a rather casual manner, which was to come back and bite me on the arse when I was serving in Northern Ireland.

I was in D Squad and my Squad Corporal was a man called Pete Young, known to all as 'Pete the Para'. He had come to the Depot as an instructor from 63 Para Squadron RCT, the Transport Support element of 5 Airborne Brigade. Pete Young was a very fit and tough man about 25 years of age. He continued to wear his maroon coloured beret, which should only be worn by soldiers still serving with Airborne Forces, but this was sanctioned to encourage recruitment of Junior Leaders into 63 Para RCT. Pete Young decided that our Squad should have a go at 'milling' – a form of boxing carried out during Airborne training. Everyone is paired off with an opponent of similar size and weight. You face your adversary on opposite sides of a gym mat and move to the left as each fight takes place. When you get to the end of the mat it is your time to fight. Pete Young was to referee every fight and if we didn't, at the very least, try to kill our opponent, we would have to go in the ring with him for the mandatory 3-minute brawl.

I was paired off with a lad called Steve Campbell. We chatted before any of the fights had started and Steve had a good idea that if we did a lot of grunting, groaning and body punches we could get through this with the minimum of pain and body damage. 'Good idea,' I thought, and readily agreed. I am not a very keen masochist. Even with this cast iron contract I was still getting increasingly nervous as we moved to the left and towards our impending personal fight. Steve winked at me as Pete the Para called us forward for our fight and we tapped boxing gloves as professional fighters do. Steve then swung a lightning and tremendous right cross straight on to my nose and all I remember for the next few seconds was seeing the universe in front of my eyes and the distinct taste of blood.

The fight then started in earnest. I really wanted to decorate the gym mat with a new colour; a shade of blood red with a hint of Steve Campbell's brain. It turned out to be the best, bloodiest and most aggressive fight of the whole session, so much so that Pete the Para suggested that we both think about putting in for 63 Para Squadron RCT when we put in our posting preferences. Steve and I became great friends.

Pete the Para also entered a team for the Nijmegen Marches in Holland and I was one of the selected few. These marches are held every year in and around Arnhem to commemorate Operation Market Garden, the allied airborne invasion of Holland in 1944. It involves soldiers from all nations marching 25 miles a day for 4 days and there is always a lot of competition and banter between soldiers of different nations. We as Junior Leaders were not allowed by the rules to wear the 25lb of webbing and one of the Yank team members commented on this, saying, "Where's your packs girls!" Dave Hand, who was on our team replied, "We dropped them in Vietnam so we could run faster, you tosspot!" Anglo-American relations hit an all time low.

Just prior to the marches, Pete the Para arranged for our team to go on a NATO Exercise in Italy with 3rd Battalion the Parachute Regiment for a couple of weeks. He thought some serious tabbing up mountainous roads in Italy would be great training in preparation for Holland.

We were taken on strength with 63 Para Sqn RCT for the whole of the exercise for administrative purposes. Billeted in Aldershot the night before flying out of RAF Lynham on an RAF C130 Hercules, we enjoyed the evening with a few beers and a great Gurkha-style curry provided by the 3 Para chefs. The curry was a real ring stinger.

The following day I boarded the Hercy Bird up the ramp at the rear of the aircraft and tried to look as nonchalant, hard and cool as the guys in 3 Para. In reality I was as excited as a dog with two dicks.

The four engines roared into life and we were soon rushing down the runway and took off into the sky in a south-easterly direction. It was at this point that I let rip with an almighty fart that smelt like an explosion in a sulphur factory. Chesh Kennedy was sitting next to me and pulled a face that confirmed his nasal senses had been violated.

"My eyes are burning!" he squealed.

If I wasn't suffering myself I would have actually felt sorry for him. The real problem was that I nearly followed through and my abdominal pains were telling me to get to a toilet without further delay as I was nearly touching cloth!

An RAF Flight Sergeant walked between the long rows of canvas seats that faced each other, each occupied by a gorilla in uniform. I shouted to him (the noise level on a C130 is so great that it is difficult to be heard without shouting) "Where are the toilets on this aircraft Sarge?" He pointed to a toilet contraption at the end of the rows of seats with a round shower curtain rail above it. "Over there lad. I hope you don't want a shit because we won't be getting a replacement privacy curtain until next week, the old one has been ripped down."

Brilliant.

We were at least another 2 hours flying time from Italy and I could already feel the beads of sweat running down the small of my back as I clenched my buttocks as tightly as I could. It was a losing battle. I had no option but to get up and use the curtain-less toilet in full view of everyone.

A huge Neanderthal Para Sergeant was sitting on the end seat no more than six feet away from the toilet. I noticed his massive fists were tattooed; the right one had 'HATE' on it, and the left had 'MORE HATE'. He noticed me and realised that I was going to use the toilet and continued to stare at me intensely. When I hesitated he nodded at the toilet and said, "Well, go on then, get on with it!"

I undid my staple belt, button and zip and started to drop my combat trousers just as Sgt Neanderthal nudged his mates and got them all to watch me. It is the most embarrassing moment in my entire life and trust me, there have been plenty.

To make it worse, as the smell spread around the aircraft, anyone who hadn't already noticed what was happening suddenly took an unhealthy interest in my bowel movement.

As I stood up after 'Operation Ghurkha's Revenge' was over, I was applauded with approximately the same gusto as General Gordon after he entered Khartoum on 18th February 1884.

The Italian barracks we were accommodated in were very basic but clean and had a tannoy system that woke us every morning with trumpet music.

I know you will think I have a toilet fixation but when I went into the Italian ablutions, in the toilet cubicles there was just a hole with two ceramic footprints where the toilet bowl should have been. 'God! Someone has nicked all the bogs', I thought rather stupidly. The doors on the toilets were like those on a saloon in a cowboy film and you could look over the top and see if it was occupied. I checked the next cubicle, which was the same, except this one had a hulking great paratrooper in residence, dropping a bigger payload than the RAF dropped on Dresden in 1945.

I realised that the Italians had a strange and uncomfortable system for emptying your bowels. This was going to take some getting used to. In the next trap I crouched down with my combats around my ankles and started to do the business that I was in there to do. All of a sudden one of our lads faces appeared over the top of the door.

"Alright Harry! You know we are on Parade at 0800 hours don't you?"

"Yeah! I know mate," I said, feeling slightly embarrassed and quite vulnerable. The young lad crossed his arms on the top of the door and continued to talk to me like a friendly neighbour chatting over a garden fence.

"So, are you going out for a pint tonight."

"Christ! Fuck off will you! I'm trying to have a crap!"

"Alright! Keep your fucking hair on," he said as he wandered off.

Another thing I thought quite strange about the Italian barracks was in the cookhouse. It had a huge glass container at the end of the hotplate that was full of red wine. The container had an orange rubber tube coming out of it so you could fill your mug at mealtimes. This wine was made available for breakfast, dinner and tea. It tasted bloody awful but the Paras seemed to like it so much they were filling up their water bottles with it.

During the day's training Pete Young pushed us harder and harder with each tab (running and forced marching). When he got going it seemed nothing could stop him. He never appeared to get out of breath no matter what speed he made us run at.

At the end of the Exercise all troops were assembled on a military range to watch a Firepower Demonstration. This included the Italian Air Force dropping napalm from some of their fighter-bombers. I remember as a child seeing the Americans doing this on news reports about the Vietnam War and thinking 'that is *awesome*'. When I saw the real thing it made me realise what horrendous weapons most armed forces have in their armouries to win battles. It was 'awesome' but it was also very scary. All the Paras just sat around on the ground making brews, talking and smoking, totally unperturbed by this amazing spectacle. I realised at that moment that British Army Airborne soldiers are the toughest and coolest soldiers you are likely to meet anywhere in the world and I came to the decision that when I was posted at the end of Basic Training, I wanted to be an airborne soldier.

But, as my mum used to say, "You don't always get what you want" and so it proved to be with that maroon beret and me. In the Regular British Army there is a small rhyme that is known by all soldiers and in particular those who have never attempted or passed Airborne Training. It goes:

"Para Para in the sky,
I didn't know shit could fly."

This is usually sung out of the hearing range of any Para, especially if you would rather not have your face rearranged.

After completing the Exercise in Italy and Nijmegen Marches in Holland I became aware that I was now a fully trained soldier, qualified to drive and maintain Landrovers, HGV 3 trucks and motorcycles. Senior Troop just needed to do the Passing Out Parade and we would all be posted to our new units.

Passing Out Parades involve the whole camp on parade but the Senior Students take centre stage. Those that are Passing Out march with fixed bayonets on their rifles. It is a formal way of moving on from a recruit/trainee to a fully trained soldier. As we formed up waiting to march onto the Parade Ground in front of our families and friends, two members of Senior Troop started to have an argument. The one in the Centre Rank was a big muscled, skin-headed bully who was disliked by a lot of his peers. I'd had a run in with him earlier in our training and I can clearly remember waiting in the queue outside the cookhouse and felt a sharp pain on my head as he belted me (from behind) with his hard plastic mug. He got a lot of pleasure out of inflicting pain on people and was the most loathsome soldier I have ever had the displeasure to meet.

He demanded that the soldier in front of him swap positions so he could be in the Front Rank and his parents would be able to see him when the Parade marched past the dais. The lad in the front rank rather rashly told him to piss off. Not one to falter at the first hurdle, the bully bayoneted his annoying obstacle in the right buttock. Blood was pouring out of him as he hopped about like Skippy the bush kangaroo and squealed like a stuck pig.

An army ambulance came tearing down column road and whisked him off to Taunton A&E Department. The bully squirmed his way out of the situation by stating the other soldier had stepped back onto his bayonet just as he leaned forward to tie up a loose bootlace and the whole incident was put down as an accident.

The Passing Out Parade went off without any further hitches and the bully's family got a good view of his ugly mug as he was moved to the Front Rank while the other guy was having his arse stitched up in Taunton Hospital.

All those who Passed Out went on two weeks leave before proceeding to their new units. I went to Aldershot for the 'Beat Up' along with six other lads and after just four days the realisation of how tough and fit you had to be to become a paratrooper was literally a slap in the face.

As a newly-qualified Crap Hat I was destined to end up at 10 Regiment RCT in Bielefeld, West Germany.

4. Learning the Tricks

West Germany. The home of some of the best lagers and sausages the world has ever seen. The fact that NASA couldn't have put a man on the moon without German rocket scientists is less important to me. I admire the German Nation for their bangers and beer.

After my abysmal failure on the 'Beat Up' I was posted to C Troop, 9 Squadron, 10 Regiment RCT, which was based in Catterick Barracks. The local town, Bielefeld, is an average size town in the centre of the Northern part of Germany and was host to five large barracks before the Berlin Wall came down. 1st British Corps Headquarters was located in Ripon Barracks about 2 miles along Detmolder Strasse from Catterick Barracks. We, as members of 10 Regt RCT considered ourselves to be the top dogs in Bielefeld Garrison. 10 Regt was made up of 9 Sqn, 17 Sqn and 36 Sqn and we were the largest (in manpower) unit in the area. 14 Sqn RCT were co-located with 1st British Corps in Ripon Barracks along with a Signal Sqn, WRAC unit and a few other odds and sods. As far as 10 Regt were concerned they were all just a bunch of handbaggers really.

Mossbank Barracks was home to a large REME Workshop and a wheeled Field Ambulance unit and the other barracks. Richmond and Harrogate were home to 6 Ordnance Battalion RAOC and Defence Medical Equipment Depot RAMC supply Depots. One of the camps was an RAOC bakery that supplied bread for a vast amount of units in our area of operations.

In Catterick Barracks I was put into a 4-man room on the top floor of one of the accommodation blocks with three other lads who had just come from Junior Leaders at the same time.

10 Regt RCT was renowned in the British Army as the Boxing Regiment. They had been Army and BAOR Champions for about 10 years on the trot. A lot of this was due to our Army

Physical Training Corps PTI SSgt QMSI Gary Fuller, who was an ABA Champion Boxer in his heyday and I believe I am the only Driver in the Regiment to have knocked him out.

At the time I was the RQMS stores truck driver and Gary Fuller was being posted back to the UK. He was at the Quartermasters doing the paperwork for his MFO (Military Freight Organisation) boxes, holding all his personal effects, to be sent back to the UK. When he had completed the paperwork he gave me a hand to load his boxes onto my Bedford MK 4-tonner so I could take them down to Richmond Barracks. I jumped on the back of the wagon, took out the tailboard pins and pushed the tailboard but it wouldn't budge. I took a step back and kicked the stuck tailboard just as Gary was coming round the side of the wagon. It shot down, hit him on the head and knocked him out cold. Being the good soldier that I was, I leapt into action and ran round the back of my vehicle holding my head and shouting "Oh fuck! He's going to kill me … He's going to fucking kill me!"

When he came round I tried to convince him he'd had an epileptic fit. I didn't get away with it and he called me a "fucking idiot". We started to load his boxes, which were stacked on pallets. When we got to the bottom box, Gary put his hands under the box through a gap in the pallet base. I couldn't get my fingers under so I gave it a bit of a kick and crushed his fingers. He said to me, "you've caused me more injuries and pain in five minutes than anyone else has in the boxing ring over the last 20 years."

You have no idea what an accolade that was for me. I had just kicked an ABA Champion boxer's arse, albeit with a 4 Tonner tailboard, some heavy MFO boxes and a pair of size 9 medium DMS boots.

One person in 10 Regt that I knew from my days in Dalton Troop at JLR was 'Flitty' Flitcroft, who was in the room opposite mine. He was posted to the unit a couple of weeks ahead of me because he was slightly older (you had to be at least 17½ years old before you could be posted to a regular working unit). We became very good drinking buddies, in fact, he introduced me to all the hot spots in Bielefeld. The Drug Store, The Buschkamp, Hans Meyer's and The Sante Fe, to name but a few of the Bielefeld night spots. I became a regular drunken pain in the arse.

Several weeks after arriving in the unit I made friends with a fellow new arrival called Fred. We went on the piss in The Sante Fe, not realising that this was predominantly a 17 Sqn waterhole and we were not welcome. After ordering *"Zwei grosse bier bitte"*, a mean-looking old sweat from 17 Sqn just along the bar growled, "What the fuck are you two wankers doing in here?" Fred replied "We're both 9 Squadron, what the fuck's it got to do with you, shit for brains?" It wasn't big and it wasn't clever. In the entrance to the bar were some cowboy saloon type doors. Fred hit the doors head-first at 30 MPH with the help of old 'shit for brains'.

I picked up Fred, trying not to get the blood from his nose over my clothes. He was very dazed. "Mum, I can't find my PE kit," he whinged.

10 Regt was full of some very tough experienced drivers. I looked up to a lot of these men, and still do in retrospect. Ray Ratcliffe, Chalky Proffit, Colin Webber, Billy Antcliffe, Kev Carter and many more were all great examples of everything that was good about the British Army in the mid 1970s. I wanted to emulate Colin Webber as much as I possibly could. He was my hero, a really confident young Scouser who seemed to know everything about driving and maintaining military trucks.

Billy Antcliffe instructed me on my HGV 2 driving course. He was the most patient and funny instructor I have ever had the pleasure to meet in all my time in the army. He was a large, jolly northerner with the biggest beer belly to be found in 10 Regt. He was about 28 years old and still a driver. Rumour control had it he had visited the Military Correction Training Centre (Army Prison) at Colchester on a few occasions and lost rank as a result. He was promoted back up to LCpl when he left 10 Regt on posting. The backbone of the British Army in the 1970s was made up of 30-year-old Drivers and JNCOs who had done time at Colchester.

I learned and passed my HGV 2 Test in an 'Old Knocker'. These 10-ton, 6-wheeled vehicles were designed and produced in the late 1940s and reflected their age when you drove them. No power assisted steering and a top (downhill) speed of 30 MPH with a crash gearbox.

In the winter of 1975 I was warned off for a detail to take Compo Rations down to Sontofen in Bavaria, South Germany. These rations were for all the troops who were taking part in Exercise Snow-Queen, the permanent skiing cadre, which I had done whilst at JLR.

We were to leave Bielefeld in the early hours on a snow driven morning after loading up at Richmond Barracks. We had a convoy of 8 AEC 10-ton Militant 6 x 6 wheeled vehicles, popularly known as 'Millies' to everyone in the Corps. These wagons were a reasonably new vehicle with power-assisted steering, good heaters and a top governed speed of 60-plus MPH. Everyone wanted to drive these beauties rather than the 'Old Knockers'. Each vehicle had a Driver and Co-Driver for this five-day trip. We would have to stop overnight at a US Army Transport Unit at Heidelberg on the way down and back.

I was Co-Driver to Ray Ratcliffe, who told me I could do the first part of the driving. I thought this was a great compliment from this tough and experienced Driver who was going to trust me behind the wheel of his trusty steed. Little did I know he was letting me go first so I would have to First Parade the vehicle in the freezing cold and driving snow.

After checking the oil, coolant, tyre pressures, lights, windscreen washer bottle, fuel, the load and restraining straps on the back I started the 'Millie' up. The convoy had been formed up on the Main Square the day before we left in the order we were to travel in. I sat there, revving up the engine whilst waiting for the convoy to move off. Ray was curled up in the passenger seat with his beret over his face, trying to take a nap. He woke up, took the beret off his face and said to me, "What the fuck are you doing? Stop revving the engine like that and pretending you've got a big dick! Nobody is fucking looking at you because you can rev-up a fucking engine! Drive this fucking thing properly or I'm coming over there to slap some fucking sense into you!"

I started driving the 'fucking thing' properly.

Several hours into the trip down to Sontofen, Ray asked me if I was feeling hungry and proceeded to get some NAAFI pies out of his travel bag. He lifted the engine cover that was between us and placed the pies, after covering them in tin foil, on the very hot manifold leading to the exhaust. Fifteen minutes later we were both enjoying piping-hot pastries that definitely filled a gap. It was better than the lousy packed meal the cookhouse had given us for the first part of our trip south. I realised at that point how much I could learn from these great blokes; they knew the tricks of the trade to improve life on Exercise and details.

The trip south was mostly by autobahn until we got into the mountainous parts of Bavaria. During these long hours of driving I got to know Ray 'Rat' quite well and my confidence in this 'old sweat' grew.

We arrived at Heidelberg in the late afternoon and were shown where to park our vehicles by an overweight black US Army MP. Some US Army drivers from the Heidelberg unit were working near where we parked up for the night. They came over to have a chat because they were interested in our 'Millies'. They seemed very impressed after being told the speed, weight carrying capacity and range of our wagons and we let them give the wagons the once over. They returned the compliment and let us look at their Dodge 6x6s that were their version of our 'Millies'. The cabins of the Dodges were open at the side as the doors had no windows and the controls and seats were very basic. The yanks assured us that they had a great Cross Country capability but I would rather have had an Old Knocker than one of these any day.

After Last Parading the vehicles (that includes refuelling, checking for leaks, damage and the load itself) we were shown the way to the Transit Accommodation block.

The Transit Accommodation was far superior to anything you would find in any British Army Camp not including, of course, the opulence of every British Army Officers Mess. After dumping our kit and rolling out sleeping bags on our beds we grabbed our 'diggers' (knife, fork and spoon) and black mugs and headed off towards the Cookhouse.

COOKHOUSE? You have to be fucking joking! This was like a *restaurant*. It was clean and tidy and not like the great big hall-type rooms with greasy floors that you got in most British Army Cookhouses in the 1970s. They had tablecloths and each table was laid out with cutlery, not dissimilar to a reasonable restaurant in the UK. The food was excellent and plentiful and when you got to the end of the hotplate you could choose between coffee, Coca-Cola, Tango, iced milk, beer, pineapple juice, root beer, apple juice, milkshakes of every flavour you could think of ... but no tea.

OK, so it wasn't perfect.

After tea we went back to the accommodation block for a shit, shower and shave ready for a night on the piss. Our American hosts would entertain us in the PX (Post Exchange) that was their version of our NAAFI (Navy Army Air Force Institute) Club. The Section Commander gave orders that at least one Driver per vehicle could have no more than two beers that night; that way one of us would be fit to drive each truck in the morning. Ray 'Rat' kindly said that as I had done such an excellent job on the initial part of the detail I should do the same tomorrow and he would set about getting pissed.

I had a great, albeit sober, night talking to some seasoned US Army soldiers who had served in the Vietnam War. I made some crass comments about looking forward to getting involved in some action against the Russian Army over the other side of the Iron Curtain. One of the Yanks said, in a Southern drawl, "Son! I pray to God you have a real boring and dull career ahead of you. You don't want to see any man die, regardless of whether he is your enemy or your friend." When you are 18 years old, soldiers who have read the book and acted in the play seem rather dull when they give out excellent advice to ignorant young lads.

We set off the following morning, after a great breakfast of pancakes and maple syrup, followed by more pancakes and maple syrup, all washed down with some of the best coffee I had ever tasted. The Americans also provided us with an excellent packed lunch to see us through till we got to Bavaria.

We arrived at the German Army Barracks in Sontofen after dark and as there were no Eager Beaver ForkLift vehicles available to unload our wagons we had to wait until the morning.

The snow was very thick everywhere you looked and the temperature was sub-zero. Bavaria during the winter is one of the most beautiful places in the world to visit, everywhere you look is like a winter picture postcard.

The barracks where we were accommodated looked just like a scene from the film 'Where Eagles Dare'; great big, dark stone block-built buildings that were probably built in the 1930s. The accommodation was old but inside the rooms were extremely clean, basic, but nice and warm. We were all put in the same large, tall-ceilinged room, which had about 20 metal bunk beds in it.

We started to unload all the vehicles at about 1000 hours the following morning once the Eager Beavers arrived and completed the task by lunchtime. We had lunch in the German Army cookhouse which included some dark heavy bread and cheese that was hairier than Giant Haystacks. We decided that we would all go down town and indulge in some Bratwurst and pommes frites mit mayonnaise. We spent the rest of the day going from bar to bar, drinking beer from huge German beer steins.

I have always been amazed at how much lager British soldiers can drink without falling over. It is a skill that can only be perfected by long hours propping up an assortment of bars in sleazy establishments and studying the subject closely. I started to get into the practice of matching the lad's pint for pint, or more accurately litre for litre. BIG MISTAKE! I cannot remember anything after we visited our fourth Gastatte. I woke up in my dossbag the following morning, stripped to my underpants with my clothes folded up on the chair on the other side of the room. I found out later that Ray 'Rat' had made sure that I was put to bed and someone was instructed to keep an eye on me.

In the morning I had the mother of all hangovers, so Ray drove all the way back up to Heidelberg whilst I slept it off. I woke up as we were driving on the autobahn with a bladder that was about to explode and I begged Ray to pull over so I could go for a piss.

"Can't," he unsympathetically replied. "We're on the autobahn and in convoy. You've got two choices mate. You can get up through the cupola cover in the top of the cab and climb onto the back of the wagon and try to piss on a Mercedes as it goes past, or piss into this and empty it out of the window trying to hit a Mercedes as it goes past."

He passed me a large empty Coke bottle he had stored behind the driver's seat, saying, "Always keep one of these in your cab. You never know when you might have to piss when you're driving."

I went for choice number two because I assumed it to be the less difficult. My bladder was giving me some gyp and I wasn't sure if I could hold back the flood whilst climbing on the cab of a ten ton truck doing 60 miles an hour. I knelt on the floor of the cab, unzipped my denims and put my knob in the bottle (with room to spare, I might add). At first it was difficult and painful to urinate because of the pressure in my bladder but when I got going the relief was wonderful. As the pain started to lessen Ray mischievously hit the brakes and, as I was holding the bottle in my left hand and my knob in the right, my face squashed up against the windscreen and I pissed over my hand and down the front of my denims.

Ray very nearly pissed himself, he was laughing so much.

The rest of the return trip was uneventful but I had enjoyed the five-day adventure immensely. This was why I had joined the RCT. I started to feel a part of the troop. In the Army you know your peers have accepted you when you walk into the NAAFI and one of the 'Old Sweats' shouts "Hey! Harry! Over here"! I loved all the piss-taking (most of which was directed at me) and the sense of camaraderie. You knew the other members of the troop would always look out for you if you were in trouble. In the same vein, they would all relentlessly and mercilessly take the piss if you had a cluster fuck.

I went on Christmas leave for a couple of weeks and astounded my mum with tales of my adventures. I'm sure she had heard it all before, having served in the WRAF as a Dental Nurse and been an army wife for many years. When, as a teenager, I had told her I wanted to join the Army, she was bitterly disappointed; she wanted me to be a carpenter and get a 'proper job'. Whilst I was on leave she became increasingly worried that I was spending so much time with a divorcee friend of hers. Veronica, or 'Ronnie' as she was more commonly known, had two children: Matthew, who was six years old and Naomi, who was three. I was to marry this woman, who was 10 years older than me, in less than a year.

No wonder my mum was worried.

I returned to 10 Regt after Christmas and prepared my wagon for the forthcoming Exercise Freeze Up. The temperature in West Germany during the winter of 1975/76 went down to a wind chill factor of minus 30 degrees. I was driving a Bedford MK 4 Tonner that was to be used as a general admin vehicle for the G1098 facilities. During the exercise it got so cold that the diesel in some of the vehicles started to solidify; they would not start without some pure alcohol cartridges that had to be pumped into the engines. Someone came up with the idea of warming up the fuel tanks of the vehicles by heating them up with the cooks Number One Burners. These blasted out a large flame like an oversized Bunsen burner lying on its side. Health and Safety? Not in 1976 mate! It worked and most of the wagons were kept running on the Exercise.

It became so cold that the OC Major Colvin arranged for the Squadron to sleep in the local Gastatte to make sure no one froze to death sleeping in the wagons. He decreed that we could all have some beers but it was to be kept to a reasonable quantity. The security of the location was to be maintained at all times with the sentry's relieved every half-hour.

I was on sentry from 2000 hours till 2030 hours when the OC came round to check on everything with the SQMS Staff Sergeant Bennett. The SQMS was a mountain of a bloke with a handlebar moustache that looked like it belonged to an RAF Squadron Leader with a Spitfire.

As the OC approached me the conversation took the following account:

Me: "Halt, who goes there, friend or foe?"

OC: "Friend."

Me: "Advance friend and be recognised."

As he approached I told him to halt a couple of paces from me and whispered the first part of the password for the night.

Me: "Green."

OC: "Man."

Me: "Evening Sir. How many are there in your patrol?"

OC: "Two, it's myself and Staff Sergeant Bennett."

Me: "Advance number two and be recognised."

As Staff Sergeant Bennett approached we went through the same routine and I made them both stand behind me.

Me: "Advance number three and be recognised."

SQMS: "What are you doing you fucking idiot? There are only two of us doing the rounds. Start switching on Clacy you fucking dimwit."

OC: "Actually Staff, he is making sure no one has tagged onto the end of our patrol and trying to break the security of our location. Well done Driver Clacy, it's good to see that someone is switched on. You look freezing cold, get yourself a piece of cardboard to stand on, it will insulate your feet against the snow and ice. How come you haven't been issued with a parka for your stag on guard?"

Me: "No parkas were brought out for the exercise Sir, I was told the SQMS thought they wouldn't be needed."

The OC looked at Staff Sergeant Bennett who was wearing a large parka.

OC: "Staff?"

SQMS: "Well … the thing is Sir … I thought that … Well…"

OC: "I think, Staff, the problem is that you didn't think. Take off your parka and give it to Driver Clacy. Hand this over to the next stag when he takes over and make sure every one on stag gets it while they are on duty. Make sure the last sentry returns it to me. Is that clear, Driver Clacy?"

Me: "Yes Sir. I feel warm as toast now. Thanks a lot Staff."

Staff Bennett just scowled at me and trotted after the OC whilst shivering in the sub zero winter temperature.

After I came off stag I went back to the Gastatte large room where we were all sleeping that night. I started to warm up after getting a brew from the large chrome tea urn that the cooks had laid on for everyone. I was detailed by my Troop

Sergeant to go into the town of Gronau at 2300 hours to pick up some lads who had spent that evening on the piss.

Before I left, the blokes who had been having 'a few beers' in the Gastatte were getting into an argument about football. It all seemed to be getting a bit nasty and an angry Staff Sergeant Bennett was in the middle of it all. Maybe the cold was getting to him. I left in my wagon to pick up the lads in Gronau and thought it would all probably blow over by the time I got back.

As I pulled up in the centre of Gronau all the lads started hurling abuse and fighting to get in the cab with me because it was so cold. They didn't fancy the freezing 15-minute journey back in the rear of the wagon.

When I got back to the Squadron location I saw a chair come flying out of a window in the Gastatte and two blokes trading punches on the steps at the entrance. It looked like the argument had blown up rather than blown over.

I climbed out of the wagon just as Corporal Dougie Allen smacked my mate Flitty Flitcroft in the mouth and sent him flying down the steps at the entrance. Flitty turned to me with blood pouring from his mouth and said, "Fucking hell! I only went in to get me fags."

Some of the tables and chairs inside had been smashed in the ensuing violence and the owner of the Gastatte was very angry and distressed.

In the morning the OC, who had spent the night at the Bugermeister's house with the SSM and had missed the whole fracas, was told that the Gastatte owner wanted a word about the previous evening's events.

When given the whole story the OC became furious. He had Staff Sergeant Bennett, who was sporting a lovely black eye, identify all guilty personnel and get them on parade wearing Nuclear, Biological and Chemical Warfare Suits. These charcoal-lined suits are worn over soldier's normal combat gear to protect against all known NBC Agents. They make you sweat if you do anything more strenuous than lying down in a cool room.

Twelve culpable combatants were paraded in the car park in NBC suits with their fighting order webbing on and carrying their personal weapons. You could smell the alcoholic fumes from about ten paces away as the Drunken Dozen swayed backwards and forwards. The OC stood in front of them and gave them the dressing down of their lives, explaining that they had let the Squadron and themselves down. He had already apologised to the Gastatte owner and explained that all those on parade would pay for the damage.

The OC pointed up the road to a stop sign and asked Staff Sergeant Bennett if he could see it. With his one good eye he squinted at the sign, which was about a mile away, and confirmed that he could see it.

"Good!" said the OC. "I want you to double these men up there and back again and you had better be quick about it".

At this point the OC shouted, "GAS! GAS! GAS!" This was the signal of a chemical attack and for soldiers to put on their respirator (Gas Mask). Whilst wearing a respirator your breathing capacity is reduced by 30%. The OC said, "Hurry up Staff, I don't want to be waiting here all day for you."

Fully masked-up, SSgt Bennett and the squad set off at a fast pace and returned about 25 minutes later, some with vomit, saliva and snot down the front of their NBC suits.

"Not quite fast enough for my liking Staff! Give everyone a drink of water and do it again," said the OC through gritted teeth.

By the time they had completed the two miles again, they all looked on the verge of collapse, with faces as red as tomatoes.

"All of you, get out of my sight!" said the OC as he headed off towards the Squadron CP.

Exercise 'Freeze Up' had been my first exercise and had been a real eye-opener; it had been bitterly cold and tiring but I had learnt a lot. To be quite honest, I was a little disappointed it was over. I felt my confidence to be able to carry out any task given to me, without making an arse of myself, was increasing all the time.

I shouldn't have held my breath!

The next big exercise was in the springtime. I can't remember what it was called but my job on this one was in 9 Squadron's LTA (Load Transfer Area). This was usually an area in a wood where loads were transferred from one vehicle to another. 10 Regiment was a Third Line Transport Unit, which meant in wartime we would collect supplies from Base Depots, then cross-load these supplies to the Second Line units for their onward progression. We would also re-supply Field Depots of the RAOC.

I was working for a Full Screw by the name of Solly, who looked like a Fijian rugby player. He was a great bloke with a really laid back attitude. My job was to guide vehicles into position by hand signals (at night this was done holding a torch) and direct the Eager Beaver forklift vehicles as necessary.

Half way through the exercise, at about 0100 hours one night, everything was quiet and no loads were coming through our LTA.

"Look Harry," Solly said. "Nothing's going on at the moment, so why don't you get your head down over by that tree and I'll give you a shout if I need you."

I didn't need telling twice, as I was totally knackered and could have slept on a washing line. I rested with my back against a tree and nodded off very quickly.

In the next hour I fell into a very deep sleep and started to slide down the incline into the LTA...

Two Old Knockers came into the LTA to be cross-loaded by our Eager Beaver and I never heard a thing. I felt something was rolling over onto the toecap of my boot and woke up to see the back wheel of the Old Knocker reversing over my feet. The pain was severe but lessened by the fact I went into shock and was still half asleep. It all seemed like a nightmare except I could hear my own screams at about 300 decibels.

As the rear wheel went over my feet I watched in horror as 22 tons of military equipment crushed them down into the soft mud. Everyone within a 2-mile radius must have heard me yell out in pain, despite the noise of three large diesel engines working at full revs. As the rear wheel passed over my feet I dragged them out before the next wheel could repeat the damage already done. I had to pull them out partly because of the suction of the mud and partly because my leg muscles were paralysed with absolute fear.

Solly and Sgt Pugh came running over and asked what had happened, I told him and said that I thought my feet were bleeding. Sgt Pugh was a First Aid Instructor; he loosened my bootlaces and told me that my feet were not bleeding and that I was going to be OK. As he put a figure of eight bandage round my ankles to immobilise my feet he sent Solly over to the CP to let them know what had happened.

The Squadron Landrover ambulance nearly ran over me as it reversed up to where I was waiting to be collected.

Sgt Pugh asked me if I wanted anyone in particular to accompany me to hospital. I asked if Driver 'Coby' Cockburn could come with me. He was sent for. I could hear Sgt Pugh briefing 'Coby' outside the ambulance on what had happened. "Driver Clacy is inside the amby because he's had his feet run over by an Old Knocker. He is in a state of shock. Go with him to the hospital and keep reassuring him that he will be OK. Any questions?"

"No Sarge, I'll look after him," said Coby.

He climbed in the back of the ambulance, took one look at me and said, "Bloody hell Harry! You look fucking awful. I hope you ain't going to die on me mate."

Why Coby never went into the nursing profession I will never know.

I was taken to the nearest Krankenhaus (German hospital) where I was assessed, diagnosed, x-rayed and treated with typical German efficiency before being put to bed for the night. An RAMC doctor came to visit me the following afternoon and made arrangements for me to be moved to BMH Rinteln.

On arrival at reception in BMH Rinteln I was seen by a doctor who read the x-rays provided by the Germans. He told me that no bones were broken and that my feet were just very badly bruised. He thought that the weight of the vehicle must have been absorbed by the thickness of the soles of my army boots, that and the soft sticky mud saved me from serious injury. I was put on 7 days light duties and given some painkillers, to be taken as necessary.

When the lads returned off exercise the usual piss-taking took place but there seemed to be general heartfelt relief that

I was ok. I could feel the warmth and compassion as someone said, “You stupid twat! You won’t do that again!”

It would not be long before I was back to full fitness and raring to get on with training for my first tour of duty in Northern Ireland.

5. Northern Ireland Training

Training for Northern Ireland tours in the mid-1970s was usually carried out at your unit's own barracks; the urban warfare training centres that units have at their disposal today were just in their infancy at that time. I think there was a set-up at Sennelager in the mid 1970s but 10 Regt never used it to my knowledge. Having said that, I think the training we all went through was very thorough and testing, to say the least.

At times during the training you had to draw on all your reserves of strength and stamina just to keep up with everyone else. Little did I know it at the time, but NI training was a good indication of how exhausted and tested I would get at some stages of my forthcoming tours.

The roads around Catterick Barracks were to be our Falls and Shankhill roads for at least a couple of months until we deployed to the real thing. At the top of the camp, by the back gate, the road ran down to RHQ, which had a large roundabout outside. On this ¼ mile stretch of road, a driving obstacle course was set up, with old wrecked cars obtained from a local scrap-yard. The guys who had completed tours of NI previously went straight on to driver training on the roads in and around Bielefeld. The Shankhill virgins like me had to complete the obstacle course in a fast time before we were allowed to hit the streets and scare the shit out of the locals.

Junior NCOs instructed us on driving the Humber 1-ton 'Pig'. They were from our own unit and had served at least one tour of duty in NI. The 'Pig' was an up armoured vehicle that had been used by the British Army in the Middle East during the 1950s and 60s. We learned how to First Parade it before setting out on a detail; this involved the usual fuel, oil, brake fluid and lights checks. 'Pigs' had Run Flat tyres fitted because even if you had room to carry a spare tyre, you wouldn't want to change one on the Falls Road, not with an

M16 Armalite pointed at you from Divis Flats. There were two seats in the front for the driver and Infantry Section Commander; in the back there were two wooden bench seats that had space to carry about eight infantrymen.

The vision from the driving seat was restricted even with the door and front hatches open. The front hatches were opened by a hydraulic hand-pump system and were located on the floor between the driver's and commander's seats.

We had to undertake driver training through the vehicle obstacle course outside RHQ with these vehicle hatches battened down. You had to look through a green tinted visor that was about twelve inches wide by two inches deep. It had a green tinge because it was made up of several layers of thick glass that made the visor bulletproof. It did make driving through narrow gaps very difficult and the wrecked cars looked even worse by the time we were competent enough to go on the public highway.

Every soldier is at the very least competent at handling his or her personal weapon, but we now had to get used to carrying our 7.62mm Self Loading Rifle (SLR) everywhere we went, 24 hours a day, even when we went for a shit. We had to load and unload our weapons every time we entered or left a building (loading bays were put outside every building on the camp); our weapons were at arm's length both night and day throughout NI training. We were not allowed to use our rifle slings in the normal manner, carrying the SLR slung over our shoulders. The sling now had to be attached to the butt of the weapon but the other end was made into a loop and wrapped round our wrists – to make sure no one could snatch our weapon away from us.

Physical Training was stepped up dramatically and included extended runs carrying weapons, Aikido, Assault Courses and Pokey Drill. This involved all Troop members standing in a circle on the main square, holding our SLRs by the pistol grip at arm's length in whatever position the sadistic bastard of a PTI instructed. The most painful was holding it straight out in front of you. A couple of minutes in this position holding a 9lb rifle soon breaks you into a sweat. If you let your arm drop before the PTI told you to change position you would get a shitload of abuse and halitosis from the Narcissistic Adonis.

Apart from learning to drive the 'Pig', the best part of NI training for me was learning how to patrol in an urban environment, commonly referred to as 'Footsies' by all RCT drivers. For training purposes, 9 and 17 Squadrons acted as rioters for and against each other. For me, many valuable lessons were learned.

On a hot sunny afternoon during training, our Troop were confronted by a lot of lads from 17 Squadron, who were acting as the 'bad guys'. We were standing shoulder to shoulder and holding them back by the block that housed the Army Legal Aid Section, next to the main square. As it was lunchtime, a lot of people were watching the action from out of their office windows. I was holding my SLR at the 'high port' (the way Lance Corporal Jones carries his rifle at the end of every *Dads Army* episode) when one of the 'Bad Guys' grabbed my SLR, thumbed the magazine release catch and ran off with the magazine. It had 20 rounds of blank ammunition in it.

"You bastard!" I shouted, as I pushed forward to grab him. The rioters parted quicker than the Red Sea when Moses was on duty. They let me through and I chased him through a gap in the hedge that surrounded the main square. The rioters then closed ranks so no one from my Troop could follow me. As I dashed through the gap in the hedge I was set upon by six blokes from 17 Squadron who, in their excitement, gave me a rather too realistic 'roughing up'. I was badly winded after receiving a size 9 Medium DMS Boot to the ribs and they all ran off laughing. This was a lesson I would remember one night during a riot outside the Royal Victoria Hospital in Belfast.

Aikido is a form of unarmed combat adapted from both Judo and Ju Jitsu that makes use of body throws and arm locks with a minimum of force. Part of aikido training involved using a Northern Ireland Riot Stick – like an old fashioned policeman's truncheon but slightly thinner and longer. We used to carry these tucked into our flak jackets with the handle sticking up from our armpit and it could be pulled out like unsheathing a sword. We were instructed that we could only strike an assailant on the ankles, knees and elbows or across the shoulders. On no occasion were we to strike anyone on the head, as we were always to use the minimum force to carry out our duties.

During Aikido lessons we were paired off on opposite sides of the gym mats (as we did for Milling with Pete the Para) wearing boots, denims, combat jackets, flak jackets and helmets. Each pair then had to take turns as the defender with the Riot Stick and then as the assailant without it. The PTI's only instruction was that the defender and assailant had to get his opposite number on the mat to win the fight – but it had to be done using minimum force only. Soldiers get very excited when they are given legal permission to beat someone into submission, particularly when they are holding a Riot Stick in their hand. Some of them got right out of hand and often grew into a full-blooded fight. One lad beat his opponent on the helmet with the riot stick as hard as he could. To be fair, he had just had his knobblers squeezed in a vice-like grip. None of the blokes taking part in these lessons seemed to understand the concept of minimum force. It was great to watch though.

The NITATT (Northern Ireland Tactics and Training Team) boys visited the Regiment from Sennelager and gave lectures in the cinema at the top of the camp. These teams were made up of soldiers, mainly from the Intelligence Corps, but who were helped by guys from other regiments like the RAOC and SASC. The lectures were the best I have ever had on any subject throughout my entire time in the army.

As we entered the cinema an Intelligence Corps WO 2 stood at the front and shouted, "Come on, hurry up and take your seats. We haven't got all fucking day!" There was a mad scramble to get a seat nearest to the front where there was an array of weapons on four trestle tables next to the stage and everyone wanted to have a look.

The WO 2 introduced himself and his team. He explained that they were there to give us an insight to the current situation in NI and hopefully give us enough advice to help us make it through our four-month tour unscathed.

He asked if anyone in the audience could pick up any weapon on the table and identify it by name and calibre. I noticed there was a US .303 Garand on the table and I stuck my hand up.

"Good!" said the WO 2, "Step forward, pick up the one you recognise and give a 30 second talk on everything you know about that particular weapon."

I started to wrack my brains about any info I could remember about the Garand and where it had been used, etc. I wanted to impress my peers. As I picked up the rifle and turned towards the audience a loud bang sounded behind me and made my ears ring and my trousers cough. It was so loud that it made everyone in the cinema jump. By the fire exit a biscuit tin had its lid blown off and they had to open the fire doors to clear the dense smoke. That was my first and last Booby Trap. The sound of everyone laughing made my humiliation even harder to bear.

We were taught about IEDs, the way IRA snipers worked, how weapons and ammunition was smuggled and what to look for in a house search. The information these guys knew about NI was endless and impressive. A lot of what I was taught I can still remember, so it must have been a very good lecture.

As a footnote to this chapter I want to tell you about a little incident that happened to a friend of mine called Taff Llewellyn whilst driver training on a 'Pig'. The 'Pigs' we used for training were not up armoured and the metal hatch above the commander's seat could be raised but not locked in the upright position. Taff was in the commander's seat with the hatch raised as it was such a hot day and had his fingers resting on the roof of the vehicle near the hatch hinges. As the 'Pig' pulled away from the traffic lights on Detmolder Strasse, the metal hatch came crashing down and crushed his fingers. He was rushed to the Medical Centre at Ripon, which was only about half a mile away and treated by the doctor before going to BMH Rinteln for surgery.

Bill Baker, who was a real London boy, was with him when it happened and drove him to the Medical Centre. Bill asked the doctor if he could speak to Taff before the ambulance took him away to Rinteln. Bill was shown into the treatment room where he saw Taff lying on the treatment couch, his left hand heavily bandaged and he looked shocked and depressed. They had the following conversation:

Bill: "Awright Taff, 'ow are you feelin' old son?"
Taff: "Not too good Bill mate."
Bill: "Wot they doin wiv your 'and?"
Taff: "They're taking a couple of fingers off."
Bill: "Fakin 'ell mate! Can I 'ave your gloves?"

This sort of humour has always been prevalent in the British Army and helped a lot of guys get through what we were going to face in Belfast.

6. Belfast

9 Squadron deployed to Belfast in an RAF C130 Hercules from RAF Gutersloh. As we were being checked in with our suitcases and kitbags I noticed a corporal from 9 Squadron standing in the queue ahead of me. He was holding just a small sports bag and his SLR. I asked him where the rest of his kit was.

"All you need for a tour in the Province are spare combats, skiddies, socks, washing and shaving kit and some civvies to go on R and R with," he replied. "You don't need most of that crap you've packed." This was experience talking. He had already done four tours of duty in Northern Ireland.

We flew to RAF Aldergrove and were transported to Moscow Camp in Bedford RLs that had been covered in Makrolon armour to protect us. Makrolon was a tough plastic armour developed by NASA to protect their astronauts in spacecraft when hit by pieces of space rock at tremendous speeds. The two soldiers at the tail end of each wagon were issued with a magazine of ten rounds of ammunition each. That, along with Saracens at the front and rear of the convoy, was our only protection.

Moscow camp was the headquarters for 9 Squadron throughout its tour and was located in the dock area on the outskirts of Belfast. When we arrived, Chris Chambers and I were told that a 'Pig' was on its way to collect and take us to our location, a base called Mulhouse, just round the back of the Royal Victoria Hospital on the Falls Road.

Before we were collected, the SQMS issued us with the extra kit we would require for our tour. This included a green motorcycle helmet that had a large and very thick visor on a frame that could be pushed up when not required, a flak jacket and ten rounds of 7.62mm ammunition for our personal weapon. For some strange reason, all RCT Drivers were only issued with ten rounds and yet the magazine held twenty. All infantry soldiers were issued with at least twenty rounds. We had been issued with our dogtags back in Bielefeld and our cap badge had been handed in so it could be painted black. The theory was that a nice shiny cap badge is a good aiming point for a sniper.

The 'Pig' arrived to collect us, driven by Glenn Wright, who had arrived on the Advance Party. He had a full screw and two Privates from the Staffordshire Regiment with him. The Staffords were the Regiment we were supporting for the first part of our tour. RCT and Infantry tours overlapped, so they would have two months to show us round and we would then have two months showing the next battalion round. Simple idea but very effective.

It took about half an hour to reach our location and I noticed as we arrived that it was covered in corrugated iron sheets and had at least four sangers covering different areas. A sanger is a sentry post built out of thick breezeblocks and has small windows with sliding thick metal windows on three sides. We turned left off Grosvenor Road onto Roden Street and then turned right towards the entrance to Mulhouse. On the left hand side was open, deserted wasteland. At night this whole area was lit up with large security lights that had been fitted by the Royal Engineers.

The sentry at the entrance dropped the thick chain barrier and we drove over it and into a rectangular courtyard that was a bit larger than the size of a football pitch. There were several 'Pigs' and a Saracen parked up on the left hand side outside the Company Standby Room.

As Chris Chambers and I got out of the back of the 'Pig' we were met by Corporal Ray Newman, who was to be our RCT Section Commander for the next 4 months. He was a tall, athletic-looking Afro-Caribbean and was a black belt in Karate. He spent a lot of his spare time during the tour doing weight training in the REME garage.

Chris and I gathered our kit and followed Ray to the corner of the courtyard by the REME garage. We went through a door and into the ablutions, then through another door into a corridor and entered the first door on the right. It was a large square room with ten beds and a couple of metal lockers, one of which had a large television on the top of it. The floor was covered in cold, beige Marley tiles. This was the RCT accommodation and our home for the next four months. Some wag had put a sign on the door that read 'Rickshaws, Camels and Taxis, just phone Green Cabs 999'. As Chris and I were the last of our section to arrive at Mulhouse, all the beds had been allocated but two. Chris grabbed the third bed on the left, which left me with, Yep, you've guessed it, first bed on the left as you entered the room. If anyone was needed for a job you could guarantee they would collar me, as I was the nearest.

As if to prove my point, the Ops Room Sergeant came into our room before I had even put my kit down and said, "We need a driver to take out a patrol in a 'Pig'. Report to the Standby Room in two minutes."

Fuck me! I had only just arrived and the Army was already hell-bent on getting me shot at. I looked at Chris but he seemed to be busy looking the other way.

"I'll take this one Chris," I said. "But if I die, I'll come back and haunt you, you ugly fucker!"

"Come on Harry," Ray Newman said. "If you are required just get on with it; the Staffords don't like to be kept hanging around."

I reported to the Standby Room with my flak jacket, helmet and SLR and found six privates and their Section Commander. He was a Lance Corporal (one stripe) and supervised us loading our SLRs. He briefed everyone on what we were doing on the patrol as I first paraded the 'Pig'.

We left Mulhouse, turned right onto Grosvenor Road and headed towards Brown Square, which was where we were to set up our mobile VCP (Vehicle Check Point). As I approached the first set of traffic lights I could see it was about to change to red. I slowed down to a crawl in anticipation of the lights turning back to green, as we were taught in training. If a gunman had us in his sights he would not be able to get a good shot at us because we were constantly moving.

I was very nervous and found the whole experience surreal. I couldn't believe that I was here, on the streets of Belfast, driving an APC carrying seven armed and lethal infantrymen.

As I pulled up into the middle of the road near Brown Square the section commander told me to close all the visors in the front of the 'Pig'. I did as instructed and got out of the 'Pig' ready to take up whichever position I was told. We were in a fairly soft area but I still dashed across the road in a crouched position and threw myself onto the pavement at the corner of a wall. The blokes in the section seemed to amble to their respective positions and one of them asked the section commander, "What the fuck's the matter with him?"

"New boy," was his weary reply.

I was trying to remember everything the NITATT boys had told me and watched every window, doorway and vehicle for possible snipers and bombers.

We spent the next three hours in and around Brown Square, stopping and searching vehicles. We took down details from the drivers' licences and noted where they had come from and where they were going. If a pretty woman was stopped, the soldier in the back of the 'Pig' taking down all the details, would sit further inside the vehicle. That way the pretty woman would have to lean inside to sign the form and the rest of the blokes could get a good look up her skirt. Four months is a long time to spend with only hairy-arsed farting blokes and no female company.

I did have some nasty company a bit later on in the tour. I can't remember exactly when it was, but one day when I returned from a patrol, Glenn Wright came up to me as I was Last Parading my 'Pig'.

"What the fuck have you been up to Harry? There's a couple of monkey's in the Coy HQ waiting to interview you."

I had no idea why the Royal Military Police would want to talk to me. Every soldier in the British Army dislikes the Royal Military Police; some are so full of their own self-importance.

After finishing my Last Parade I headed off to the Coy HQ. The Stafford's CSM showed me into the OC's office where two men in grey suits were sitting behind the main desk. I walked over to them and said, "Afternoon, I'm Driver Clacy, I believe you wanted a chat with me."

The larger of the two men said, "SIR."

"You don't have to call me sir," I replied. "I'm just a Driver."

You could hear the tumbleweed crossing the room in the deathly silence.

"I'm a WO 2 in the SIB and you call me SIR! Is that clear?"

Bloody hell! I thought. *What have I done? These blokes seem really pissed off with me and we have only just met!*

The interview took the following course:

Me: Sorry Sir I didn't realise, as you are both in civilian clothes." (The other monkey seemed embarrassed by his mate's outburst)

WO2: "Are you 24316524 Dvr Clacy?"

Me: "Yes … Sir."

WO2: "Do you have a bank account at the Commerz Bank in Bielefeld?"

Me: "Yes Sir."

WO2: "Did you withdraw some money two weeks before coming to Belfast?"

Me: "I don't know … probably, why sir?"

WO2: "As customers withdraw money from their accounts the slips are serial numbered in a franking machine in numerical order. The man in front of you on that day had just forged a slip and had stolen some money from another soldier's bank account. We want to know who that soldier was?"

Me: "I'm sorry sir, but I just can't remember; it was about two months ago."

WO2: "So you can't remember anything, Driver Clacy. Then how come you know it was two months ago? I didn't mention what date the crime was perpetrated on?"

Me: "Well sir, you asked me if I had withdrawn money from my account two weeks before coming out to Belfast and that was two months ago."

The WO2's questioning technique must have been taught at the Inspector Clouseau College for Dimwits. He seemed to be getting very angry and sarcastic at the same time.

WO2: "Oh, I see! I think I know what happened on the day in question. I think the pair of you were in it together. What did you do, split the money fifty-fifty?"

Me: "I'm sorry sir, I wish I could help you with your enquires but I really can't remember."

He started shouting and banging the table.

WO2: “The only one who is going to be sorry, Driver Clacy, is you … when we send you to prison in the MCTC at Colchester for fraud.”

It was at this point that the other monkey, who I think was a Staff Sergeant, stepped in and suggested his mate step outside and get a breath of fresh air. The Staff Sergeant then took over the questioning as the ‘good cop’. It was an exact copy of a script from a Starsky and Hutch episode, except the acting was slightly more appalling.

I don’t know if they got their man or not, but if they did it wasn’t with any help from the sharp eyes and photographic memory of Driver Clacy.

❖ ❖ ❖

Our Squadron was in Belfast during the Orange Day Parades on 12 July 1976. These Parades were a celebration by the Protestants in Ireland to commemorate the Battle of the Boyne. On 1st July 1690, James II lost the throne to William of Orange and both sides raised armies and fought on the banks of Boyne River. King Billy won.

Back to the 1970s and the city of Belfast was segregated into different areas for Catholics and Protestants. The British Army erected large concrete barricades on some of the roads that crossed into ‘enemy’ territory. These chicanes stopped vehicles speeding into and out of any given area and a sanger in army locations usually covered these border-crossing points.

Each Company in the resident Battalion had a designated area to cover in Belfast. During the Orange Day Parades this involved long hours standing guard on crossing points between Catholic and Protestant areas.

We were all called out one day as a riot had started outside the Royal Victoria Hospital at the junction of Grosvenor and Falls Road. I turned left onto Grosvenor Road from Roden Street and took place on the far right of four ‘Pigs’ that were slowly driving abreast of each. As we drove at a crawling pace up the hill towards the Falls I could see the RVH on the left and Dunville Park on the right. Dunville Park was a grassed area with a few flowerbeds and paths, surrounded by an iron-railing fence.

I could see hundreds of rioters on the Falls and a couple of hijacked cars that had been set on fire spewing out lots of black smoke. Some of the rioters were trying to push a hijacked flatbed lorry down the hill towards us. I was told by the Section Commander to halt the vehicle and wait about half way up the hill, the other three 'Pigs' halted at the same time. We were level with the centre of Dunville Park when I noticed a mob of rioters cutting through the park on our right. They were heading straight for me, with the intention of denting my head with house bricks. I wasn't sure which was going to be the biggest problem, the flatbed lorry or the rioters. The lorry started to roll down the hill but veered to the left and came to a stop on the kerb before it could pick up any speed. I looked back at the rioters in the park and noticed they were starting to back off and were running up towards the Falls Road. It was only then that I noticed a Sergeant had grabbed half the guys out of the back of our vehicle and was charging towards the rioters. We continued up the Grosvenor Road and turned right onto the Falls, still with all four 'Pigs' abreast. It was formation driving at its best; the Royal Signals White Helmets motorcycle display team would have looked on in awe.

The rioters had backed off down the Falls and were about 50 meters away, but running towards us, throwing missiles and running away again. We were instructed to halt the vehicles and all the infantry debussed and formed a formidable line in front of the 'Pigs'. They had large clear Makralon shields that not only gave protection against missiles but also was effective against acid and petrol bombs. They held their ground against a furious barrage of bricks and rubble. I got out of the 'Pig', as I didn't want to miss any of the action. The adrenaline rush was incredible.

Just behind the frontlines of infantry were soldiers armed with 1.5 inch FRGs (Federal Riot Guns) which fired rubber bullets. These were used to break up formations of rioters at a distance of 25 to 50 meters; they inflicted shock and bruising but were not designed to cause serious injury. Soldiers were trained to fire the rounds so they bounced off the road to take some of the force out of them. I watched the FRGs being loaded with rounds that were carried in old, 58 Pattern water bottle carriers on their belts. The front guys parted the shields just enough to allow the FRGs to be fired at the rioters. I saw one rioter hit on the knee as the round bounced off the road and he collapsed I could see he was screaming with the pain. The FRG teams reloaded their weapons as some rioters ran forward in a heroic charge to pick up their wounded comrade but the guy who was hit on the knee seemed to be waving his mates away as if saying, "Leave me! Just go and save yourselves." As the second salvo of PVC headed down the road, followed by a snatch squad of soldiers armed with riot sticks, he got up rather quickly and, in fact, overtook his mates as he ran for safety.

The snatch squad came back with a rioter and threw him in the back of my 'Pig' and secured his hands behind his back with plasticuffs – a thin plastic strip that was looped around the prisoner's wrists and secured through a one-way buckle. The only way to remove them was by cutting them off with wire cutters. An infantryman was detailed to guard the rioter in the back of my 'Pig'.

Soon another rioter was thrown into the back of my vehicle we were told to take them to Tac HQ (Tactical Headquarters) at Castle Street to be processed and interviewed.

I reversed the 'Pig' back to the junction of the Falls and Grosvenor Road and backed into Springfield Road. The two prisoners were flanked by a couple of Staffords. One of them looked quite scared but the other was mouthing it off about us all being "British Bastards" and we should all "Fuck off back to where you came from!"

He was asked, very politely, to "SHUT THE FUCK UP!"

We arrived at Castle Street, the guard on the gate lowered the chain barrier and I drove over to reception and followed the prisoners and escorts inside. Each prisoner had to be accompanied at all times by his arresting officer. When a soldier arrested a suspect he had to place one hand on the suspect's shoulder and say, "In the name of her Majesty's Forces I arrest you." He would then have to write a statement at Tac HQ of the events leading up to and during the arrest and could at some stage, depending on the circumstances, make a court appearance with the suspect and give verbal evidence.

The scared-looking one was taken to an interview room by a couple of uniformed soldiers and the mouthy one was left standing with his back to a wall with his arresting officer. A short, stocky, dark-haired man wearing civilian clothes and a Magnum PI moustache came and stood in front of him and looked up into his face. Magnum PI then punched the arrested man right up and under the ribs. He collapsed onto his knees and started retching as he tried to get his breath back. I was really shocked by this. I couldn't believe the British Army would deal with a prisoner in this manner. We were the good guys. It was a real eye-opener for me.

As the four of us left to return to the riot, I heard the rioter sob in his broad Belfast accent, "Yer moight make me croy, but yer wown't brayke me, yer barstards!"

The riot continued throughout the day and was one of the most exhilarating times of my life. It wasn't a war zone but it was about as near as I was ever going to get in my career as a soldier.

At about midnight we were sent up to North Howard Street location in four 'Pigs' with about 30 infantrymen. The 'powers that be' wanted to flood the ground with plenty of troops to prevent any trouble before it started again. Glenn Wright, Chris Chambers, Bruce Cunningham and I were driving the vehicles; we went to the RCT accommodation on the top floor of a multi-storey building to see our mates. The Staffords went to a briefing and were accompanied by Glenn, as he was the senior Driver amongst us. During the briefing he was told all RCT were to wait in location when the Staffords went out on the 'Footsie'. They didn't have the time to wet nurse a few 'Trogs' (Infantry slang for RCT Drivers) out on the streets.

Glenn went ballistic. I don't know exactly what he said but we went out on the patrol with them.

We patrolled back up the Falls to Springfield Road near the RUC Station and set up a 'Footsie' vehicle and personnel checkpoint. A drunken middle-aged woman approached us and was asked by a soldier to 'open her coat'. We wanted to make sure she wasn't carrying anything illegal underneath it. After she told him what he could go and do with himself, he pointed out that he would have to hold her there until a 'Coffee Pot' could be brought to search her and that could take up to 45 minutes. She made a great fuss before realising we were not going to let her go until we saw the inside of her coat.

A cursory inspection of her coat after she took it off revealed nothing and we let her continue up Springfield Road, whereupon the old cow picked up a dustbin lid and started banging it on the pavement, shouting "British Bastards! British Bastards!" It wasn't long before the streets started to flood with plenty of people hell bent on making life interesting for anyone in a British Army uniform. We backed down the Springfield Road towards the Falls under a hail of rocks and petrol bombs. Luckily, I was at the back of our patrol and wasn't hit by any of the missiles.

A Full Screw next to me said to his section "This one lads" and moved into a shop doorway and started to kick the door in. *Good idea.* I thought *He's obviously trying to get some extra cover for his lads and that was why he is taking these extreme measures.* I was such a naïve 18-year-old. Once inside the shop he gave the order, "Quick, fill your pockets, we haven't got very long before that lot get down here." The blokes in the section all turned their torches on and started filling up a patrol bergen with booze, fags and chocolate. It looked like a convention of burglars were holding their Annual General Meeting in this small Belfast shop.

"What the fuck are you doing?" I said. "This is against the law! You could all get in a lot of trouble."

"When that lot up the road find this place open they will strip it like a bunch of fucking locusts and they will get the blame," the Full Screw replied. "So either fill your fucking pockets or wait outside!"

I waited outside with my RCT mates, who also didn't take part in the robbery.

When I came to Northern Ireland I thought I was coming to save the Irish people from tyranny. I saw myself on a white charger with my sword drawn and raised above my head ready to take on the evil protagonist's.

Yeah, I know, what a fuckwit – but that was how I felt.

After returning to North Howard Street when everything had quietened down we mounted up into the 'Pigs' and started to drive back to Mulhouse. As we approached the junction of Grosvenor Road and the Falls we saw some young lads throwing stones at the front of the RVH.

"PULL UP AT THE FRONT OF THE HOSPITAL" the section commander screamed. "PILE OUT LADS … AND GRAB THE BASTARDS!"

I pulled on the handbrake, grabbed my rifle and chased after one of the yobs as he ran down a side street. As I turned the corner I saw him disappearing into the dark, past the only working streetlight. I started to slow down, as I was on my own and I remembered what had happened in training when the lads from 17 Squadron pinched my magazine. I knew that if I was grabbed by this lot I would get a lot more than 'a bit of a roughing up'. I noticed four or five lads re-grouping in the shadows and discretion became the better part of valour. I retreated back to the 'Pig'. Not one of the little sods was caught and we returned to Mulhouse empty-handed.

Just before the Staffords handed over to 1st Battalion of the Light Infantry, who were the next Roulement Battalion, I was to learn a very important lesson about doing my job properly.

I was on a routine patrol on the Falls in a 'Pig' when the engine died and the ignition lights came on. I coasted to the side of the road and put the handbrake on. The section commander asked what the problem was and I told him I didn't know.

"Get this fucking heap moving," he told me, "because that's Divi's Tower over there and I don't want a sniper having a pop at us." As the section deployed onto the streets and took up defensive positions I turned over the engine but it would not start. The engine on an APC is a sealed unit and there was not much you could do on the street if it broke down, it really needed the help of a mechanic in a workshop.

I told the section commander to get on the net and request 'Bluebell' (Codename for REME mechanical assistance) to attend at our present location. Another 'Pig' from our location turned up about half an hour later and our REME VM (Vehicle Mechanic) got out with a couple of Jerry Cans of petrol and a funnel. I looked at the petrol gauge, which on 'Pigs' were notoriously inaccurate and it was reading about quarter full. The VM looked at me from the section commander's side of the 'Pig' after he had checked the petrol tank on his side. It was bone dry. I unscrewed the petrol tank cap on my side; drier than James Bond's Martini.

Harry Clacy was definitely shaken and stirred at that moment. It was, and probably still is, a military crime to run out of fuel as an army driver.

I hadn't actually First Paraded the 'Pig' before we went on patrol and obviously the last Driver to use it hadn't Last Paraded it either. That is not an excuse either, because if I had First Paraded it I would have seen the tanks were not full. If I had done my job properly we wouldn't be in this embarrassing and dangerous predicament.

The section commander looked over the VM's shoulder and asked if it could be fixed. My heart was beating ten to the dozen. The VM winked at me and said, "I think there is an airlock or some dirt in the system, it's quite common on these engines. I'll flush it out with some fresh fuel."

He put both Jerry Cans of fuel into the petrol tank on his side and switched the fuel tank change lever over towards his side. I thanked the VM profusely – out of earshot of the section commander – and he said, "Anyone can make a mistake Harry, just don't do it again mate."

The section commander didn't believe a word of what the VM told him and kept throwing me some hostile glances.

We finished the patrol and returned to Mulhouse for lunch. I reverse parked the 'Pig' outside the standby room as usual, we always reverse parked for a quick deployment and we all unloaded our weapons in the loading/unloading bay.

"Alright lads," the section commander said, "go and get some scoff and be back in the standby room in half an hour."

He then pointed at me with a black padded-gloved hand and looked very angry. "I want a word with you in the bogs."

I walked into the empty ablutions next to the RCT room and noticed the red tiled floor was wet from recent cleaning. I turned around to apologise to the section commander and all I saw was a padded-gloved left hook coming towards my nose at a hefty rate of knots. I flew backwards and, not for the first time, tasted blood in my mouth. I came to my senses as the section commander pulled me to my feet by the shoulders of my flak jacket. I mumbled my apology as I was thrown against the back wall.

"The fact that you are sorry doesn't mean a fucking thing to me," he said through gritted teeth. "The fact that you could have got any one of my section killed today because you can't be arsed to do your fucking job properly does. I can't prove it was your fault we broke down, but if it ever happens again, I promise you, I will fucking kill you!"

He stormed out of the ablutions and slammed the door behind him.

I washed the blood off my face and the front of my flak jacket and went back outside to Last Parade the 'Pig'. After completing this task I went back to the RCT room for the remaining ten minutes of my lunch break and sulked on my bed whilst everyone was busy elsewhere. Glenn Wright came in the room, took one look at me and said, "What's happened to you, you look fucking awful." I told him I had just been smacked about a bit by one of the Stafford's. He wanted to know who it was so he could go and give him a bit of a slapping – Glenn was a bit of a hard case – but when I told him the full story he ripped me to pieces verbally and confirmed what I already knew. I had got everything I deserved. I pointed out that whoever had driven the 'Pig' before me had failed to Last Parade it and was partly responsible for what happened. Glenn pointed out that if I had done my job properly the RCT in our location would only have been embarrassed about *one* wanker, not *two*. He had an idea who had failed to Last Parade the 'Pig' and had a sharp word in his ear. I took it on the chin – or more accurately on the nose – and never again took out a vehicle on a detail without thoroughly First Parading.

vvv

When the Light Infantry took over from the Staffords the day-to-day routines carried on in much the same vein. When you were on duty in the standby room you were in there for twenty-four hours and were basically there as a QRF (Quick Reaction Force). We had to respond to any emergency that was notified to our Ops Room. There was a small hatch from there into the standby room and details could be given to the section commander without any delay. Everyone on duty had to remain fully clothed, with boots on, ready to move at a moment's notice.

One thing we had to respond to several times a day was Operation 'Rat Trap'. Two sections from every location in Belfast would deploy to predetermined positions, seal off the city and try to capture any terrorist who had just carried out illegal activities. A very loud alarm bell would be the sign to get your flak jacket on, load your weapon and deploy on the ground as fast as you could. Adrenaline would surge round your body as you woke from a sleep and burst into action any time of the day or night from the Standby Room. It was probably very effective, but personally I never saw any results from these emergency callouts. Every time that bloody alarm bell used to go off it was so loud I nearly shit myself!

I did think we had caught some terrorists one-day. We were carrying out a VCP in the middle of the road outside the ABC cinema in Belfast city centre. I was given the job of checking driving licences and searching the suspect vehicles. A Ford Cortina was directed into the VCP – that was the area in between two parked 'Pigs' – it had four large, unshaven and greasy-haired blokes inside. They all looked extremely hard and dangerous. I had the feeling I was looking right into the face of the IRA.

I asked the driver for his driving licence, which he handed over. In 1976 the driving license in Northern Ireland was a small, blue, book-type document about the size of a box of Swan Vestas matches. When I opened it there was an old battered British Army Identity Card inside. The driver didn't even look at me when he said, "Do not search the boot of this car." I was unsure what to do so I went over to the sergeant who was out with us on this duty. He ran a check on the car and was told to wait out. He told me to give the car a cursory inspection and follow the driver's instructions and leave the boot alone. As I looked round the car and inspected under the wings the sergeant talked to the driver and received instructions over the radio. I was told to let the vehicle go. After it had gone I asked the sergeant, "What was that all about?" He told me that the blokes in the car were SAS and 14 Intelligence (14 Intelligence Company worked closely with the SAS, carrying out Sneaky Beaky undercover work). He thought that they probably had a stack of weapons and ammunition in the boot.

A lot of what we did in Northern Ireland was mind numbingly tedious, interspersed with moments of excitement and humour. I returned from patrol one day and found Bruce Cunningham lying on his bed, reading a letter. Bruce was half Australian and half Scottish on his father's side and therefore had dual nationality. Whilst bumming around the world he had arrived in England without a penny to his name and decided to join the British Army for three years to solve his insolvency. He joined the RCT because he wanted to get a couple of HGV licenses while he was at it. Bruce had the bed next to me in the RCT room. He chuckled as he read his letter, so I said, "Good letter Bruce?"

"Yeah!" he replied. "Great one mate. Do you want it back?" He was reading a letter my girlfriend at the time had sent me!

He was a great bloke who had a hundred and one stories on every subject. After his four-month tour he would have plenty more to talk about. One day while he was patrolling in a 'Pig' round some derelict houses off the Grosvenor Road he was bombarded by milk bottles filled with white paint. Some teenage lads had thrown them from an upstairs window. As Bruce had been driving with the hatches open he was covered in white paint. He was lucky it wasn't acid.

He pulled on the handbrake and ran into the building with his SLR and charged upstairs to confront the 'Barrstards' that had done this to him. By the time the section had followed him upstairs he had the young hooligans lined up against a wall and, sitting on an old crate, had the first one over his knee and was giving him a good spanking.

When he brought the 'Pig' back to Mulhouse we cleaned the white paint off with some paint stripper and the acidic chemicals also took off some of the green paint that normally covered it. Underneath we found the 'Pig' covered in sand coloured paint and a unit badge in the form of a palm tree with a camel. These colours and unit badges dated back to the 1950s and 60s when they were used by the RASC in the Middle East.

I had about one month of my tour left when I was detailed to take a 'Pig' to Divis Tower. There was an OP (Observation Post) at the top, from which troops could spy on the entire city of Belfast with powerful telescopes and binoculars. A replacement soldier had to be taken up for one who was going on compassionate leave. I had been to Divis flats many times before to drop off and pick up troops who were switching duties, but I had never been up to the top of the tower myself, as I had to stay with the vehicle. On this occasion I asked the section commander if I could take the replacement up and bring the other guy down so I could see what it was like up there. He and his section had been up the tower plenty of times and were not particularly interested in who went up there, so I was given permission.

The two of us got into the four-person lift and pushed the button that would take us to the top floor. About half way up the lift started to slow down and eventually stopped and the lift doors opened. Outside the lift stood two rough and nasty looking blokes who could easily have ripped our heads off and pissed down our necks.

Shit, I thought. *What the fuck do I do now?*

I cocked my SLR so it was ready to fire, pointed it at the pair of them and shouted, "Stand back, Security Forces!" (just in case the uniforms, weapons and helmets didn't give it away). To my surprise they both backed off straight away and said they would catch the lift on its way back down.

We continued up to the top floor and when we turned right out of the lift I noticed a grey Fire Escape type ladder securely bolted to the wall. At the top of the ladder was a square metal hatch leading up onto the roof of the tower. On the wall was a small doorbell button to announce our arrival. I rang the bell and we both climbed the ladder after one of the lads opened the hatch. On the roof there were some green waterproof ponchos anchored to the walls with some green string. They were at about waist level and stretched out to give some cover from the weather for some sleeping bags. The lieutenant in charge of the OP welcomed the new guy and told the guy that was leaving to get his kit together. While the departing bloke got his kit organised I went and had a look over the five-foot sidewalls that ran round all sides of the roof. As I peered down at my matchbox sized 'Pig' at the base of the tower I could feel my sphincter go into spasm.

In the corner of the roof area I noticed a pile of coiled rope that was anchored to the roof with a couple of D shackles. A Lance corporal explained that it was there in case someone decided to set fire to the top floor to try and incinerate everyone. If the choppers could not get to them because of smoke or bad weather they would throw the rope over the side of the tower, climb down to a lower level and smash through a window to safety. I took another look over the edge and nearly shit myself at the thought of what these blokes might have to do to save their own lives.

I could not get off the top of Divis Tower quick enough.

My first tour of Northern Ireland was an amazing experience. I learned a lot about my friends, myself and how I fitted into the grand scheme of an Operational Tour with the British Army but one particular part of my first tour I will remember for the rest of my life. I can't remember exactly when the following took place, you must bear in mind it was thirty years ago, but the memories of the incident itself are forever etched in my brain.

I was driving a section in a 'Pig' and approached an incident in Leeson Street, near a place nicknamed 'Armalite Corner', so called because of a crude painting of an M16 rifle on the sidewall of a house. We approached the area just after a 'Footsie' had been attacked with an IED (Improvised Explosive Device). I pulled up on the right hand side of the road behind two other 'Pigs' that were parked side-by-side and, blocking the road, I grabbed my rifle and stood guard by the front right wing of my vehicle. I looked up the road and saw two soldiers lying on the pavement; they had both been injured by the IED when it had been detonated. The injured soldier nearest to me was screaming in pain and had his leg elevated by one of the soldiers treating him. He had lost his foot and part of his lower leg. Just before he had a First Aid Field Dressing put over the wound, I was mesmerised by a small amount of bloody flesh hanging down from the muscle on his lower leg, which seemed to sway backwards and forwards every time they moved his leg.

At the time I remember thinking, 'Who has done this? Why have they hurt these blokes? They didn't do anything. They came over here to stop the violence and some callous bastard has blown his foot off!' I felt physically sick. They were both taken away in a Saracen Ambulance and one of the 'Pigs' that were parked in front of mine. I was told the injured soldiers were either from the location at North Howard Street or Albert Street Mill. Rumours later circulated about their fate but I never found out conclusively what happened to the pair of them. I don't think I really wanted to know.

Later on that day I was alone as I sat on my bed in the RCT accommodation cleaning my rifle. There is a catch by the butt of the SLR that you move to 'Break the Weapon', this means that the rifle will pivot in the middle like your leg does at the knee. This is done so you can remove the top cover and working parts and give the inside of the rifle a good clean. As I looked at the stripped down rifle on my lap I noticed my hands were trembling. I felt my throat was closing up and my eyes started to water. I started to shake uncontrollably and I began sobbing like a child left alone in the dark. The tears and snot that streamed down my face fell onto my rifle and I tried to wipe it off with the cuff of my combat jacket. I didn't know what was happening to me but I felt like a frightened child and I wanted my mum. I wanted my dad to come in shouting and swearing; he would sort everything out for me. By the time some of the lads came into the room I had regained control of myself and washed my face. I pretended to be asleep as they laughed and joked about something childish.

I have often wondered how many times this happened to young soldiers over the years, and not just in Northern Ireland. It is a hard macho world in the British Army and it could not operate if it had to stop every time someone wanted to have a cry. I had to get on with it like everyone else.

This was the harsh reality of Belfast in 1976.

7. Who'd be an RSM?

I applied to get married just before the Squadron left for its tour of duty in Belfast. In those days you had to write a Demi-Official letter to the OC requesting a formal interview. When the SSM marched me into the OC's office, I halted in front of his desk and saluted. He asked the usual prevalent questions like, "Why do you want to get married?" and "How long have you known this woman?" I was surprised when he asked if he could see a photograph of the 'suspect' I was intending to marry. I showed him a photo of Ronnie, who had Matthew and Naomi sat on her lap. "Please tell me these are her nephew and niece," said the OC. I explained that Ronnie was a divorcee, that she had divorced her ex-husband for adultery and that she had two young children, aged six and three. The OC grilled me about the responsibilities of marriage and about taking on two children when I was still only a teenager myself. He reluctantly gave his permission but urged me to think long and hard before I went ahead with taking on these heavy responsibilities.

After I had marched out of the OC's office, the SSM went back in and shut the door and spoke to the OC. I imagine his first words were along the lines of, "Have you got the Welfare Officer's telephone number on speed dial sir?"

Both 9 and 17 Squadrons went on block leave for a couple of weeks after getting back from their tours of duty in Northern Ireland. We had a couple of weeks in camp, waiting for flights home, and spent a lot of time sweeping up leaves on the vehicle parks and picking up fag butts. During this period I got reacquainted with an old mate I had first met in Morley Troop JLR in Taunton; his name was Johnny Walker and he was from Pimlico in South West London. He was a small lad with a hare lip and a hooked nose that he could squash flat to his face, as it had no bone in it. Johnny was the funniest man I have ever met in my life. He was known as Gonzo (the Muppet with the long, hooked nose and squeaky voice) by just about everyone in 10 Regiment. Johnny became a very successful Regimental flyweight boxer. My kids would grow to love this man as much as I did. He often used to talk about his times with the 'Chelsea Head Hunters', who were the 'firm' of Chelsea Football Club.

About six of us went on the piss in Bielefeld one night as we kicked our heels waiting for our flights home on leave. As we got more and more drunk in the 'Drug Store', a young Turkish lad who had been eyeballing my mate Kevin Norton, dashed over and slapped him in the face and ran out of the club. Now, you have to bear in mind that Kev was a dark-haired, muscular and very hard young Londoner who was borderline psychotic. He looked a lot like a young version of the actor Jack Palance and had had an unhappy childhood growing up in the tough area of Brixton where his prison officer father was posted. We all knew Kev was not right in the head because he was a Queens Park Rangers supporter.

As he scrambled over the table we were sitting at, pushed past us and pursued his attacker, Johnny shouted, "Stop him!" I wasn't sure if he was referring to the Turk or Ken but either way we all joined in the hunt. Outside I saw Kev and Johnny chasing the bloke up the street heading towards a club called Cicero's, which was a drinking club frequented by young men of Turkish origin.

At the entrance of the club the Turk dashed in, closely followed by a very angry Kev. Johnny stopped at the door, looked back at the chasing pack and shouted "COME ON!" He then charged inside, punching and kicking anyone with even a hint of Middle Eastern ancestry.

The Turks had initially stood back in shock as two Kamikaze Londoners re-enacted the invasion of Gallipoli in 1915. Kev and Johnny had put marginally less thought and preparation into their attack than Winston Churchill had into his. I saw Kev's feet sticking up over the top of the table he had dived over to get at his assailant and I could see his elbow moving up and down as he pounded the face of, presumably, the young lad who had initially assaulted him. As the other three lads and I ran inside the bar, the words of Alfred, Lord

Tennyson – 'Into the valley of death rode the six hundred' – immediately sprang to mind. It was a running battle, of which there was only one likely outcome. We were outnumbered by at least three to one. We did a tactical withdrawal as Johnny dragged Kev out of the bar by his neck. He was still trying to punch and kick anyone he thought deserved his undivided and violent attention.

The following morning I saw Kev going for a shower. He was wearing a towel wrapped round his waist. His whole body was covered in bruises and abrasions. "Morning Harry. Fucking good laugh last night!" he said, in a cheerful manner. I only had a fat lip and grazed knuckles but felt like I was dying. He was such a hard man.

I flew back to the UK with Glenn Wright, who was coming to the wedding. He would eventually give Ronnie away at the wedding (a pity he didn't give her away to someone else). I had known Ronnie for at least ten years but had not spent more than a couple of weeks at a time with her. I realised she had a negative and depressed attitude towards everything within two weeks of marrying her. My father, who had divorced my mum by now, attended the wedding, but Ronnie didn't think we should ask my mum, as she felt she held some sort of animosity towards her. Her feelings were totally unfounded but I was to learn over the next twenty years of marriage to Ronnie that she could 'read between lines'.

After the wedding at the local registry office we had a brief honeymoon at a cheap London Bed and Breakfast, paid for by my dad. One night we went to Wormwood Scrubs to meet Dad and his new wife, Jill, to go out for a meal together. As we sitting round the table, waiting for our food to arrive, the restaurant burglar alarm went off and it sounded like the alarm in our standby room back in Mulhouse location in Belfast. I stood up and reached out for my SLR and screamed in Jill's face, "WHERE'S MY RIFLE! WHERE'S MY FUCKING RIFLE!"

I had been responding to that alarm for four months and automatically went straight into to 'Operation Rat Trap' mode. My dad grabbed my arm and said, "It's alright son, calm down, what's the matter?" I felt such an idiot when the

Indian restaurant manager came over and asked if there was a problem. Dad explained that I had just come back from Northern Ireland and there was nothing to worry about. It was a really strange incident.

After the period of leave was over, I returned to 10 Regiment and applied for a Married Quarter so that Ronnie and the kids could come over and join me. I was called off the Vehicle Park one morning and told to report to the Troop office. I hoped I had been allocated a Married Quarter but my Troop Sergeant told me I had to report to the RSM in Regimental Headquarters.

I couldn't think why a low life like myself should be summoned in person to such hallowed ground.

The RSM's Office was upstairs in RHQ, directly opposite the top of the stairs. A corporal from the Pay Office told me the RSM was in the CO's office and that he would be back in a couple of minutes. I stood to attention at the side of his office door and waited. RSMs in the 1970s were fearsome blokes. If you saw one marching around the camp you would see soldiers scurrying around corners to get away before he pointed his pace stick at you and started shouting and screaming. The most popular phrases that came booming out of their mouths were:

"Get your haircut!"

"Put that beret on properly!"

"Do that button up!"

"Put that fag out!"

"Stop fucking mincing and start fucking marching!"

"Did your mother throw out the baby and keep the fucking afterbirth?"

All in an affectionate and friendly manner, of course!

"Who are you and what do you want?" the RSM growled.

"I'm Driver Clacy, C Troop, 9 Sqn. I was told to report to you Sir."

"Oh yes, come into my office." I marched into his office and stood to attention in front of his desk.

"Do you want to be an RSM one day?" said the RSM. I told him I wouldn't mind having his wages for the month. "Do you want to be an RSM?" he repeated, through gritted teeth. After confirming that one-day I hoped to achieve the top position of RSM, he replied, "Good! Report to the TCO (Transport Control Officer) of 36 Squadron and pick up the rubbish truck. You are now the Regimental Shit Mover."

The rubbish truck was an old Bedford RL tipper truck that had a superstructure and canvas cover the same as the troop carrying type. It was possible to elevate the main body of the vehicle and tip out the rubbish by means of a hydraulic pump, powered by the engine. The job of 'Regimental Shit Mover' was actually quite a doddle. I was my own boss and as long as I emptied all the dustbins around the camp, no one ever bothered me (although that may well have had something to do with the fact that I smelled like a Victorian dustbin). It was hard work on a Monday morning, though; the dustbins were always overflowing with empty food wrappers, beer bottles and discarded porno magazines, usually with the pages stuck together. Squaddie weekends rarely varied.

I had been doing the job for about two months when the TCO informed me that Driver Ainsworth was to take over from me. He had to work with me for a couple of days to learn the locations of all the dustbins around the camp and where the landfill sites were. We reported to the Pay Office and picked up a chit that had to be handed in every time we dropped a load at the landfill site. The 'Obercrappen-sitenfuhrer' who worked at the landfill site in Bielefeld used to say to me, *"Kein Chit, Kein shit"* (No Chit, No Shit).

We had about half a load of garbage in the truck and as I was passing 9 Squadron accommodation block I decided to show Ainsworth where the bins were on the other side of the main Drill Square. As I turned left onto the square I saw the whole Regiment on an RSM's Parade with the Commanding Officer stood on the Dais at the front, ready to take the salute when they all marched past. The RSM blew a fuse the moment the tyres of my rubbish truck defiled his Parade Ground. He started waving his pace stick in a threatening manner and told me to "GET THAT HEAP OF SHIT OFF MY PARADE GROUND BEFORE I FUCKING JAIL YOU CLACY!"

I put my foot down and accelerated as quickly as I could to get off the parade ground and drove behind the CO's dais.

Ainsworth quickly stood on the engine cover and stood to attention out of the cupola hole in the roof of the cab and did a smart salute to the CO as we drove past. The CO returned his salute and pirouetted whilst doing his impression of a guppy fish as we shot past the back of the dais. I was told later that the canvas on the truck was flapping about like Batman's cape and through the acceleration all sorts of rubbish was flying out of the back of the truck.

Once Ainsworth took over the duties of Regimental Shit Mover I went back to 9 Squadron vehicle park. I went back to the UK at some stage to pick up Ronnie and the kids after I had taken over a Married Quarter at Oerlinghausen. It was a third floor flat with three bedrooms and when I took it over Glen Wright accompanied me as my adviser. He had been married and lived in Married Quarters previously. Staff Sergeant Bennett, my Squadron SQMS, was the outgoing occupant of the flat and had to hand it over to me. When he saw I was taking over the flat he said, "If I knew it was you taking over I wouldn't have bothered cleaning it." I got the feeling he didn't like me. The Estate Warden who was going to mediate between Staff Bennett and me on the hand-over/takeover was WO1 Ron Ross, of the Royal Artillery, a huge, barrel-chested Scotsman who had served over 22 years in the British Army.

"If you hadn't cleaned the flat Staff, I would be giving you a very large bill for cleaning it," he growled. He then winked at me and said, "Shall we get on with it Staff."

I loved Ron Ross, he was such a great guy.

The flat was large, immaculately clean and I was sure Ronnie would love it, as she was living in a shitty prefab council house in Braintree that had been built in 1946.

I flew back to the UK and brought my new 'instant' family over to Bielefeld. Ronnie and I both agreed that the kids would not be put under any pressure to call me 'Dad' – the decision was to be left up to them. When we landed at RAF Gutersloh I was holding Matthew and Naomi's hands as we walked down the mobile steps to get off the aircraft. Naomi said, "When are we going to Germany?"

"We're already *in* Germany, aren't we Dad?" Matthew replied. From that point onwards I was 'Dad' and they were the best parts of my married life.

My best man at the wedding was my mate Dave North. We had shared the same room before I got married and he had come from the JLR to 10 Regiment at the same time as me. He was a very smart and intelligent soldier who the OC of 9 Squadron requested as his personal driver. Dave came up to me one day at NAAFI break and told me the OC had nominated him to be put on a Regimental JMQC (Junior Military Qualification Course). All soldiers had to complete this course before they could be promoted to the giddy heights of the rank Lance Corporal, the first rung on the career ladder to Field Marshal. Dave told me that the course started the next day and that someone from 9 Squadron had dropped out because of an injury.

I was working in the Squadron servicing bay at the time and, as I queued up to get my NAAFI pie and pint of milk, I was wearing oil-stained overalls and my face was smeared with axle grease.

"Perhaps I could get on the course with you, mate?" I said.

He laughed and said "If you don't ask you will never know."

I left the NAAFI and headed off to Squadron Headquarters to see if I could nominate myself for the course. The headquarters was deserted except for the Admin officer, Captain Andrews. I marched into his office, saluted, and asked if I could have a quick word with him. I explained that I had just heard about the vacancy on the JMQC course and wondered if there was any chance of me being put on it. He told me to sit down and he phoned the Training Wing to find out if the vacancy had been filled. It hadn't.

The Squadron headquarters started to fill up with personnel returning from their mid-morning breaks and the new SSM (Squadron Sergeant Major) was one of them. WO2 SSM Maher was a massive, dark-haired Welshman with an Action Man scar on his left cheek. He was known as 'The Bear' and feared by every man that met him. He used to tell everyone that the only man he ever respected was the man who gave him the scar on his face. That man was a Scottish Lance Corporal called Jimmy from 17 Squadron, who stood about 5 foot 6 inches in his army boots.

Legend had it that 'The Bear' was a very drunk guest in the Corporals' mess one night and was swearing in front of some of the corporals' wives. Jimmy told him respectfully to leave the Mess as his behaviour was out of order. He offered Jimmy to come outside and try to sort it out, if he was man enough. Jimmy led the way out of the mess, followed by 'the Bear'. As he walked out, Jimmy picked up the lid of a dustbin that was just outside the door and when 'The Bear' was outside Jimmy dustbin-lidded him in the face and knocked him out cold. He then calmly walked back into the Mess and arranged for someone to take the unconscious Bear to the Medical Centre.

I stood to attention and trembled as Captain Andrews explained to 'the Bear' about the vacancy on the JMQC Course and told him he thought I should be put on it.

"I know plenty of men I would put on the course before *him*, sir," said the Bear.

"Well they haven't had the temerity to knock on my office door and ask to be put on the course Sarn't Major, so I'm putting Driver Clacy on it. Take the rest of the day off Driver Clacy and prepare your kit for the course."

I went to the Training Wing to find out what kit I required and was allocated a large locker to keep it all in for the duration of the course. Dave North seemed pleased that I had been accepted but hadn't thought it would happen.

"When you went to see Captain Andrews you looked a right fucking state," he said.

I wasn't bothered what 'the Bear', Dave or anyone else thought, I was on the course and determined to do well, as I wanted to progress up the promotion ladder. I had a new family to provide for and didn't want to be left behind by my peers.

All JMQC Courses in the British Army are run on roughly the same syllabus and organised and administered by your own unit instructors. The Training Wing Sergeant at 10 Regiment was a good Senior NCO who was an expert in Drill, Weapon Instruction and NBC (Nuclear Biological and Chemical Warfare). We were going to be taught how to drill a squad of men, how to give lessons in weapon training and a host of other things that you need to be able to do as a Junior NCO.

I reported to the Training Wing the following morning and paraded outside with the other students in a heavily-starched uniform and bulled working boots. Dave North looked immaculate, as usual. The Training Sergeant did our first inspection and sent a lad off to the Guardroom to be jailed for not standing closer to his razor whilst shaving and having fluff on his beret. He was marched away at double time and held in the Guardroom for half an hour, buffing the polished floors, whilst the rest of us were marched around the Drill Square at double time until we were sweating buckets.

I wondered what I had let myself in for.

Every day a new Duty Student was appointed from the Course members, whose duties included making sure the whole squad was in the right place at the right time for lessons and any parades. The Duty Student also had to march everyone to and from anywhere we had to go. Soldiers are used to being drilled but it is a different kettle of fish when you are suddenly put in the front of a squad and have to give the words of command. You become very self-conscious, especially when all the other soldiers in the camp who are not on the course start wolf-whistling and taking the piss. I remember one poor bastard who was caught by our Training Sergeant taking the piss. He had to join us on the Drill Square for a whole lesson and then had to stand out in front of the squad and drill us. He made a total arse of himself and our Training Sergeant told him to fuck off before he threw him in jail or put him on a JMQC Course to make a proper fucking soldier out of him.

The course was very hard work but great fun. I thought I would struggle, as everyone seemed to be more intelligent and smarter than me, but I did start to excel at taking Skill at Arms lessons and developed a real flair and desire for instructing. It was something that, in my later army career, I was complimented about on many occasions. We learned how to make out lesson plans that had to be followed when giving a Skill at Arms lesson. These lesson plans had to be handed in to the instructor after the lesson was completed. We were marked for accuracy of content, neatness and, of course, the actual lesson itself. Over the four-week course every student took at least eight practice lessons on a mixture of the SLR, SMG or the 9mm Browning pistol. My lesson on the test day was SLR Lesson 8, which was about the loading and unloading of the weapon. It was a doddle and I got top marks out of the whole course. Dave North struggled a bit on instructing, as he always got a bit flustered when having to talk in front of a group of soldiers. He would automatically start to blush and lose track of what he was supposed to be telling us.

Dave used to come to my flat at night and we would work on our lesson plans, bull our boots and give our Skill at Arms lessons to Ronnie, Matthew and Naomi, to practice our instructing techniques. They were all armed with brooms and mops borrowed from various neighbours. My new family could all have become very competent weapon specialists by the time we had completed the course.

In the flat below mine lived a WO2 SSM in charge of the Royal Signals unit in Ripon Barracks. He was called John and only expected me to call him 'Sir' when either of us were in uniform or in the presence of any superior ranked person. He came up to my flat at night for a few beers and inspected Dave's and my uniforms and helped us with our drill. He said it was better than sitting in his flat listening to what sounded like a stampeding herd of wildebeest above his head! Dave and I both appreciated the time and help that John gave us.

On the Drill Test each student had to stand in front of the squad and put them through exactly the same drill movements. These included a series of movements around the Square, with and without weapons, saluting and slow marching. This was all done in front of a Board of Officers that usually consisted of the Adjutant, Regimental Sergeant Major and the 2ic of the Regiment. They all carried clipboards and marked us on smartness, correct words of command, clarity of voice and the squad's responses to our commands. It was quite nerve-wracking but I came in the top three on the course.

When my friend Johnny Walker did his JMQC Drill Test he stood in front of the squad with the Board of Officers watching. His words of command were:

IN OPEN ORDER … RIIIGHT … DRESS!
EEEEEEEYYEEES … FRONT!
MOVE TO THE LEFT IN THREES … LEEEFT TURN!

Johnny then burst into song and started singing,

BYYYY THE RIGHT…
OF THE SILVERY MOON
NOT THE SUN BUT THE MOON
I'LL WANT TO CROON…

He was sent to the guardroom and jailed for about half an hour for messing about but was let out to complete and pass his Drill Test after the board of officers had stopped laughing.

Only one person on our JMQC Course failed, he had struggled on the Skill at Arms lessons and Drill Test. I felt sorry for him but was elated that I had come in the top four students on the course. It gave me a lot of confidence in all my abilities as a soldier and I started to be aware of my appearance and conduct at all times.

Dave North was promoted to Lance Corporal shortly after completing the JMQC Course. Some of the lads said he only got it because he was the OC's Driver. That may have been partly true, but Dave was still a switched-on soldier who outstripped most of us in smartness and knowledge of Military Driving. The OC was issued a new Land Rover and Dave set to work getting it ready for the next Brigade Exercise. He sorted out his scrim (camouflage) nets and hessian skirt (a cloth skirt that goes around the vehicle and when unfurled conceals the shape of your wheels and covers your headlights and brake lights). These are all important points when trying to hide your vehicle from the enemy when in the field. He then checked his toolkit and First Aid kit, to make sure they were in perfect order, and also put together a very good comfort pack for him and the OC when out in the field. This included washing bowls, brew kit, chocolate bars and biscuits. Dave wasn't a toady with the OC; he was just very good at his job.

I went back on the vehicle park after the JMQC Course and had been assigned a 'Millie' 10 Tonner that I had to get ready for the up and coming Exercise. Dave pulled up in front of my 'Millie' in his new Land Rover and asked me if I wanted to go for a cabbie round the camp in it. I agreed and Dave shot off at a hell of a speed. He flew off 9 Squadron vehicle park, past the Squadron HQ and along the cobbled road outside the Corporals Mess – a long, straight piece of road that ran the length of 9 Squadron vehicle park and had a left-hand bend at the bottom that took you back round the other side of the square.

Dave was a very good driver who liked to drive at high speed. He dropped the Rover down to second gear and accelerated round the corner and up the inclined road at about 25+ miles per hour. It was at this point that the door of the Land Rover sprang open due to my weight and the centrifugal force of the cornering vehicle. I wasn't wearing a seatbelt and fell out of the Rover and rolled over and over until the security fence stopped my unexpected departure.

Dave screeched to a halt and came running up to me.

"You made a boot mark on the OC's door as you fell out!" He could see I wasn't seriously injured and shouted over his shoulder as he strode back to his beloved new Land Rover, "Get up and clean the mark off the door!"

I was lucky I only had a few bruises and a sore elbow.

The exercise was hard work and we spent a lot of time on the road picking up simulated loads of ammunition, rations and POL (Petrol, Oil and Lubricants). At one stage I had three huge rolls of Royal Engineers field landing strips equipment on the back of my wagon and a trailer hooked on the back with another three rolls. It wasn't a particularly heavy load but it was massive. I arrived at a crossroads next to the location where I had to drop the Royal Engineers kit in the early hours of the morning. I was instructed to turn right and drive up the hill and find a field on the left where other vehicles were parked and get my head down until I was called forward at first light. There were no streetlights on the road and you can't drive into a unit location in the field with your head-lights on, so I parked on the hill, grabbed my SLR and did a recce on foot. I walked into the field and had a quick look around but couldn't find any other wagons, even though there were tyre tracks from other Military HGV vehicles all over the place. I went back to my wagon and carried on driving up the hill and down the other-side. The road started to narrow quite considerably, so much so that the only thing that could get past me on that road would have been Naomi Campbell, but only if she slimmed down a bit.

On the left side of the road was a very narrow, fir tree lined dirt track that had a deep and narrow ditch at either side of the entrance. If I reversed into that, there would be no way I could drive out again and no way could a REME recovery vehicle get past me to pull me out. When I looked at the map, the road I was on just seemed to fizzle out about 3 kilometres further on. I got out, looked at the track, paced it out in foot-steps and checked it against the width of my 'Millie'. There was only about a two-foot margin for error on either side of the entrance where the narrow ditches were. I got back in the wagon, drove past the track and put on the four-way flashers to shed more light. I could just make out the track in my left-hand wing mirror. I put some right lock on the steering wheel and started to reverse, the trailer started to head in the right direction down the track, I reversed the lock on the steering wheel and the wagon started to follow the trailer. I stopped several times and got out to check that the trailer and wagon were not going to drop in the ditch, I made it down the track inch perfect and headed back up the road from the way I had come. As I didn't have a co-driver on the Exercise, there was no one to witness this bit of precision driving with a massive load and trailer in virtually pitch-black darkness. I can hear all my ex RCT peers shouting 'so fucking what! I've done better than that whilst wearing a blindfold'. I'm putting this story in to show that the driving skill of RCT Drivers in the 1970s was very good because of the high standards expected of everyone within the Corps.

I drove back to the field and did a more thorough recce and found some very well scrimmed-up Bedford RL's parked up at the side of the field under some large trees. As David Niven said in the Second World War propaganda film *The Way Ahead* – "Time spent on reconnaissance is time never wasted."

I've mentioned before, health and safety in 1976 wasn't a high priority in the British Army; you just got the job done the best you could. There were no tachographs fitted in army vehicles. If a detail came in, whoever was available was sent out on it, regardless of how long they had been working or how many miles they had already clocked up. I had been on the go for over 24 hours with only a catnap of about an hour when six 'Millies' were detailed to go to Pombsen to pick up a load of simulated ammo. Pombson was an RAOC ammunition depot that held real ammunition for if the Russians came over the border and simulated ammunition for Exercises if they didn't.

I was third in line of the convoy and, after being loaded up with eight pallets of ammo, I secured the load with the large web restraining straps each wagon was issued with. Whilst working and walking about in the open air, my tiredness seemed to be lifted somewhat but I was still so knackered it seemed hard to concentrate on what I was doing. The Lance Corporal who was leading this particular convoy briefed all the Drivers after loading up and gave us the grid reference and Tac Sign numbers to follow of the receiving unit's location. Tac signs were small tactical road signs put out by units to direct visitors to their location.

As I was the third wagon and very, very tired I didn't bother paying too much attention; I would just follow the wagon in front of me. We had been driving for about 20 minutes when my eyes began to close. My eyelids seemed to have hundredweight cement bags hanging on to them. I opened the window and started taking deep breaths of fresh air and slapped myself in the face in an effort to stay awake. Even splashing water on my face from my water bottle only helped momentarily. We stopped at some traffic lights at a set of crossroads in a small village and I thought I would just close my eyes for a couple of minutes while we waited for the traffic lights to turn back to green. I woke up five minutes later with the three wagons ahead of me somewhere else in West Germany and the traffic lights back on red. I hadn't got a clue where they had gone and I was so tired that I couldn't think straight. My left-hand indicator was flashing and I seemed to remember the wagon in front of me had been indicating left when we pulled up at the lights.

'Fuck it,' I thought. 'I'll turn left and hope and pray that it is the right direction.' The guy in front of me should have been looking in his wing mirrors and slowed down until I caught him up. That was the theory of convoy driving. The reality was that he was probably as exhausted as me and he hadn't even noticed that the three other trucks had disappeared from the convoy. The two wagons behind me followed as I pulled away from the traffic lights. I went hell for leather and eventually caught the others up at the next village. Phew!

Sometimes luck is on your side.

This sort of thing was common in the 1970s when driving on exercise with the RCT. Some of the Drivers in other units were not so lucky and ended up in ditches or piling into German civilian cars because of sheer exhaustion. In the late 1980s the 'powers that be' devised a method to be used on exercise by all military drivers to make sure they got enough sleep and cut down on the accidents. It was a very crude form of a tachograph and soldiers being soldiers, it was open to abuse, so you could wangle a couple more hours' shuteye.

I loved being an RCT Driver and looked forward to every exercise and detail that came my way. It was all going to come to an to an end, though, after another tour of Northern Ireland, this time with 17 Squadron in South Armagh.

8. South Armagh

My next tour of Northern Ireland was going to be in Newry, South Armagh. British Soldiers referred to South Armagh as 'Indian Country'. The tour would involve a lot of rural patrolling of the border crossing points with Southern Ireland and this was reflected in our training. I had to learn about helicopter drills and how to drive and maintain the Alvis Saracen APC, known by all RCT Drivers as 'Cans'. These were the main APCs used in South Armagh. My ginger-haired instructor in Bielefeld was a Mancunian called LCPL Cyril Tickle. I wouldn't laugh too loud at his name, though; he was a martial arts blue belt and as hard as nails.

He took us through how to First Parade the 'Can' before we took it out on the streets of Bielefeld on Driver Training. In addition to the usual fuel, oil, hydraulic fluid and tyre pressures checks we also had to pump the Gear Change Pedal (GCP) ten times in each of the five gears. The GCP was in the same place as a clutch pedal is on a family car. Sounds easy enough, but the resistance on a GCP was similar to leg pressing on a multi-gym apparatus with the peg set on 200kg. Just in case you can't do the maths, that is fifty leg presses with your left leg. If you didn't do this on your First Parade you could end up with what was called a False Neutral. The GCP would fly upwards, further than it normally would, with a great deal of force when trying to change gear and as there was a metal strut behind both feet, it could trap your left foot. It required considerable strength to push it back in due to the fact the driving position in a 'Can' is very confined. If this happened whilst travelling downhill at 50 MPH, panic could set in quite quickly, particularly with the nine passengers in the back.

It was a pre-select system. You selected 2nd gear to start off (1st gear was only for very steep hills) with a small metal gear lever on the floor on the left hand side, push in the GCP and let it out in one swift movement. You could feel the vehicle lurch forward but it was held in place by the handbrake, the gear lever would be put into 3rd gear as the handbrake was released and the vehicle was accelerated away. When the right speed was reached the GCP was pushed in and released to put the vehicle into 3rd and the gear lever put into 4th gear and so on until you reached 5th gear. Once in top gear you selected 4th gear with the gear lever straight away ready to change back down when required.

On the right hand side of the driver's seat on the floor was a small lever next to the ratchet handbrake. When pulled backwards it put the transmission into forward drive and when pushed forward it put the transmission into reverse drive. The Saracen therefore had five forward and five reverse gears.

The steering wheel was in the opposite position to that in a normal vehicle; the upper part of it was nearer to you than the bottom part, it was impossible to cross your arms whilst driving a Saracen, you had to push and pull as you turned corners.

On the left-hand side of the driver's seat was the C42 radio that we had to learn to tune and operate and on the right were the battery boxes; both made for a very confined driving position. The seat was like Virgil Tracey's entrance into Thunderbird 2 – a large green vinyl seat that pivoted backwards. The back of the seat rested on the floor of the vehicle, allowing the driver to get in position before the seat was put back in the upright position.

In front of the driver was a small hatch, similar to the ones in a 'Pig', which could be opened by a hydraulic pump. If the hatch was in the closed position a large emergency escape hatch could be pushed open on its hinges at the bottom. It would lie on top of the engine covers. This was mainly used by Drivers to get in and out of the Saracen after parking up whilst out on patrol.

All Drivers had to go through intensive Weapon Training on the .30 Browning Machine-Gun that was fitted in the turret, in location in NI the RCT would be responsible for the daily cleaning, maintenance and fitting of the weapon and ammunition to the 'Can'.

On my first Driver Training lesson with Cyril I noticed that the 'Can' drifted left and right without moving the steering wheel. He criticised me and told me I was driving like his granny after she had taken her Mogadon sleeping pills. However, once I got the hang of the vehicle I was driving like a Boy Racer on Speed. We got to drive on the tank tracks on Sennelager training area. We chased each other round the area through muddy tracks with massive puddles. At some stages I saw Saracens with all six wheels off the ground as they were driven over hillocks at 50 miles per hour. I have never been on such an exhilarating ride before or since. Disney World could learn a lot about scary rides from some of my old RCT mates. The 'Cans' were put through the high-powered wash-downs after Driver Training to clean them.

We also did a lot of driving round the streets of Bielefeld, which included night driving. The reasons for this were two-fold. Firstly, the British Army in NI operated 24 hours a day and we therefore did a lot of night driving on the Tour. Secondly, the streets of Bielefeld were less congested at night and that reduced the chances of bending someone's BMW.

Whilst on night driver training one night, Cyril made us drive down to the Euro Centre – a brothel in the middle of an industrial estate. I pulled up in the car park outside and there were at least half a dozen 'Cans' parked up with a group of ten soldiers stood around smoking, talking and having a bit of a laugh. The rest of the blokes were inside, helping out the West German Economy by spending 50 Deutsche Marks each. Inside was an open-air square with a few shrubs in the middle. Around the edge was a path so that clients could walk round the square, look into the small, dimly-lit rooms and choose which 'lady' they were going to enjoy for the next few minutes. Some wag shouted, "MOUNT UP! QUICK, THE MONKEYS ARE ON THE WAY!" It was really funny to see soldiers diving out of the rooms, pulling up their combat trousers, thinking the Royal Military Police were doing a raid on this out-of-bounds area.

Everyone got the chance to fire the .30 Browning from the turret of the Saracen. When it was my turn I got into the vehicle and noticed the smell of cordite and hundreds of spent brass cartridges on the floor. I stood up in the turret and saw the .30 Browning bolted into its cradle, next to the weapon was a box of .30 ammunition that was again held in its own cradle. I was in a 'Can' on the far right of four others all being used for firing practice on the army tank range, 100 meters ahead of each vehicle was a wooden target of a tank. Standing on the catwalk at the side of each turret was a weapon instructor who gave advice and instructions throughout each firing session. There was a periscope sight that had a white round circle with a white dot in the middle for the main aiming point, after loading the weapon I fired about thirty rounds at the target in front and then went through the unloading drills. I was a bit disappointed when I had to unload the Browning as I really wanted to fire off all 250 rounds in the ammunition box.

Helicopter training was something new to me, as I had never travelled in one before. The RAF came to the sports field at Catterick Barracks with three Wessex helicopters that we could play with for a couple of days. We went through a safety briefing by the aircrew of the choppers; this included never going round the rear of the aircraft (to prevent you losing your head in the rear rotor blades). Everyone was also instructed to never approach a helicopter after it had landed until given the thumbs up by the pilot.

We loaded up in the Wessex and went through the crash drill of putting our weapons on the floor under our feet and linking arms, ready to brace for an impact. The Wessex took off, flew around for a couple of minutes and came back to land on the football pitch, where we all disembarked. We then all got back in the chopper and went through the same flight but when the Wessex came back into land it hovered about 10 feet above the ground. We then all had to jump out and assemble at the edge of the football pitch. On our third flight everyone had to climb down a thick rope that was suspended from a shackle above the cabin door, the rope was only about 40 foot long but it seemed a lot higher. We had to sling our weapons over our shoulders before we climbed down. I was the last to leave the aircraft and could see my mates at the edge of the football pitch looking up and hoping I was going to make an arse of myself. The pilot of the Wessex helped me do exactly that by lifting the chopper and taking up the rest of the slack rope that was on the ground as I was descending. I fell off the rope before I reached the ground and landed in a very undignified heap to shouts of "Fucking Dope on a Rope!"

After we had completed NI training we had a brief leave before deploying to the Province. My wife said she'd had a premonition that I was going to get hurt and that I should be very careful. No shit Batman!

I can't remember anything about the trip out there but when I arrived at our location in Newry I noticed that all the 'Cans' were parked out on the main road outside our location. A Sanger was right next to them so a sentry constantly overlooked them. We entered the location through a double corrugated iron gate into a small courtyard about the size of a tennis court. A sentry controlled who came in and out of the location. I met our Section Commander, Corporal John Chowanski, a small, wiry balding chap who talked in a quiet and very calm manner. He looked, and was, very fit. He had served in 63 Para RCT and still wore his Para Wings on his shirts, jumpers and combat jackets but was the antithesis of most people's idea of what a Paratrooper is like.

We entered the main building and passed the cookhouse that was on the ground floor, climbed the steps up to the upper floor and walked to the end of a long corridor. The Royal Marines Detachment room was at the end and the RCT room was on the left hand side next door. I went into what was to be our home for the next six months; a four-man room that housed twelve men. There were four sets of triple bunks against the walls, a couple of steel lockers and a square table covered with an army blanket in the middle of the room, a television set was on top of one of the lockers. With six .30 Brownings and boxes of ammunition in the corner it was very crowded. The only light came through a small 4ft by 3ft window in the top right hand corner of the room, the top of one of the sets of bunks came level with the window. The room smelled of oil, sweaty feet and farts. We were taking over from 8 Regt RCT, who were based at Munster, in West Germany. They envied 10 Regiment's name as 'The Fighting Tenth' because of our prowess in the boxing ring. One of their departing Drivers had scrawled across the wall in large letters 'You call yourself the Fighting Tenth! Well, fight the boredom in this fucking hole'.

For the first part of the Tour we were supporting the QLRs (Queens Lancashire Regiment) or, as they were more popularly known, the 'Quick Let's Run' or 'Queens Last Resort'. The second part of the tour we were supporting the 2nd Battalion Royal Green Jackets, the tour would cover the Christmas period of 1977/1978.

We spent a lot of time on the Dublin Road at the old customs post carrying out mobile VCPs (Vehicle Check Points). On my first patrol I went down to the 'Can' with the following equipment that we needed for every patrol:

1. Head and Handset for the C42 Radio.
2. External Aerial for Radio.
3. Driving Helmet with intercom system.
4. Flak Jacket.
5. Personal Weapon (SLR) and Ammunition.
6. .30 Browning Machine-Gun that weighed 30lb.
7. Box of 250 rounds of .30 ammunition.
8. Fixing Bolts for the Machine-Gun.

To first Parade the 'Can', we had to set up the aerial and tune in the radio, then bolt in the Browning and load it with ammunition. We had to be outside at least 15 minutes before the Infantry. At some time during this tour, Driver Mark Ratcliffe and I were put on a charge by one of the Infantry Sergeants, who was new to our location. We were usually outside 15 to 20 minutes before the Infantry, setting up the 'Can' and yet we usually ended up waiting another 10 minutes before they showed up ready to start the Patrol.

Over the following weeks we got used to the Infantry's tardiness and refined our timings in accordance with them, which was when we were 'Warned for Orders'. For this particular patrol the Sergeant in command came out early with his section and started to lose his rag at us straight away.

"Why the fuck are we having to wait for you fucking cowboys?" he started to rant. "We should be mobile by now!"

Mark, who wouldn't look out of place as a strongman in a circus, said in his strong Liverpool accent, "Weer alllwaaeys ouwt eer aeearly. Weer yewsually waytin fer yew fokin lot."

It didn't go down well and he was told to shut his big mouth before it was filled in. When we got back from the patrol the Sergeant took us to one side and told us he intended to charge us with being late for a parade. No matter how much we explained to him about how things were normally done, he would not listen.

The OC of 17 Squadron came down from the Squadron HQ in Long Kesh to Newry to officiate our charge. He was given a small room by 2 RGJ in which to interview us. As we waited outside, Mark told me to leave all the talking to him as he had been charged quite a few times and knew all the legal format that needed to be followed. This was the first and only charge of my entire Army career.

After the OC read out the charge and statement from the QLR Sgt he asked us if we had anything to say in response to the charge. Mark said, "Wee didn't doo nuttin fokin wrong ser! Dey arrr joost a fokin boonch of fokin twwaatts … ser!"

Now, I don't have a legal mind, but I felt Mark was not presenting a good case for the Defence.

I gave the OC my interpretation of the events leading up to the charge and he seemed to be happy with my statement. He told us that he had considered all the evidence and was going to admonish us in regard to the charge. He asked if we understood what that meant.

Mark stated, "Yeah! Wee didn't dew notin fokin rong sir!"

The OC explained that was not the case, but there was an element of doubt in the whole affair and we should consider ourselves under a warning. He also advised us to make sure we were always ready to go on patrol in plenty of time regardless of how the Infantry conducted themselves.

Several weeks later, I noticed a Full Screw from the QLR's Recce Platoon coming in the front gate with a large plastic bag in his hand. He looked like an old tramp. His face and ears were covered in camouflage cream, his hair was matted and he stank like a mad woman's shit. He had been on OP (Observation Post) duty for about a week, overlooking the Derrybeg Estate. This involved sitting in a camouflaged 'Hide' in the ground. It was usually just big enough for two men, who would observe a particular house for any terrorist movement. An OP was usually built and moved into at night only. If the 'hide' was built properly, most people could be stood right next to it and not even know it was there. Those in the 'hide' had to eat, urinate and defecate in an area the size of an under-stairs cupboard. All faeces, urine and any rubbish were taken away with them in plastic bags and bottles after their mission was completed.

I asked the Full Screw what was in the plastic bag and he said, with a cheesy grin on his face, "Do you want to have a look?" I shrugged my shoulders and he opened the bag and took out the gutted carcass of a mongrel dog about the size of a Border Collie. Dogs in NI were a pain in the arse for soldiers on OP duties as they could sniff out a 'hide' and give away the location to the local inhabitants. This unfortunate animal was wandering around alone and started sniffing around the observation slit of the OP. The Full Screw had thrust his hand out, grabbed the dog by its collar and dragged it into the 'hide'. He had then plunged an SLR bayonet into the dog's stomach and up into its heart, killing it almost instantaneously. He told me they had to be extracted from their 'hide' soon afterwards. People came looking for the dog and he felt that they might be compromised and wanted to get away before that happened.

When 2 RGJ took over from the QLR nothing really changed except for the faces. One face in particular I shall never forget was a nasty piece of work called Sergeant Brewer. He seemed to hate most things in life, probably because he was a short-arsed little runt, but he seemed to hate me most of all. Whilst out on a mobile VCP he was the Patrol Commander. I was stood in the turret of the 'Can', manning the Browning and doing car checks on the radio as they came through our location. He came in the back of the 'Can' and asked if I could operate a GPMG (General Purpose Machine Gun), a 7.62 mm, medium size, clip link fed weapon used by all infantry battalions. Stupidly, I told him that I could operate it. He told me to pick up the GPMG that was in the back of the 'Can' and follow him. I followed him for about 30 Meters away from the VCP to a ditch that ran alongside the road. It was a very cold but sunny day and the ditch was half filled with water that had a covering of ice on the top.

"You're to cover the VCP from here. Get in the ditch," he said. I lay down at the side of the ditch and said I thought I would be all right from there. He gritted his teeth and growled "I told you to get in the fucking ditch, now fucking get in there!" It appeared that negotiations were not an option. I jumped into the ditch breaking the ice. The icy water made me gasp for breath as it came up to my bollocks, which retreated up into my chest for some warmth. He told me I would be relieved in about 15 minutes and to keep my eyes peeled at all times.

Forty minutes later, as my teeth were chattering away like a demented Morse Coder, I heard someone from the VCP shouting "MOUNT UP! WE'RE MOVING LOCATION!" I couldn't bend my legs to climb out of the ditch; they felt as if they had seized up due to the ice-cold water around my knees. Two Riflemen came over and helped me out of the ditch, slid me into the driving seat in the 'Can' and pushed it into the upright position ready to drive. The warm air coming through from the engine eventually put some feeling back in my legs but it was quite painful and difficult to drive.

Why this Sgt disliked the whole world so much is beyond me but one thing was for sure, I would get my revenge on him. It would take pure luck and about two years of waiting, but I would get my revenge when I was posted to Tidworth.

About four weeks into the tour with 2 RGJ the operational procedures on mobile VCPs changed because of increased terrorist activities. We now had to man 24-hour VCPs; the section that was on duty would patrol up and down designated roads and put up VCPs at irregular points. The relieving section would deploy in Land Rovers, bringing jerrycans of fuel to re-supply the 'Cans', RV (rendezvous) with the section being relieved and they would drive the Land Rovers back to the Location for their rest period.

It was during one of these handover/takeover periods that I met with an accident that was to change my life forever. We had taken over at 2200 hours and I was refuelling the 'Can'. The returning section had taken the fuel funnel back with them so I was improvising with a traffic cone. The filler cap on a 'Can' is just above the catwalk on the right hand side of the vehicle but because the traffic cone wasn't an exact fit some of the fuel had spilt onto the catwalk and made it very slippery. The last thing I remember was screwing the filler cap in place, my legs slipping on the catwalk and falling backwards. It was at this point that a car was trying to break through the VCP. I remember seeing the flash of a headlight and feeling a sharp pain on the right side of my head before instantaneous unconsciousness.

I was told later that the sentry with a GPMG on the edge of the VCP jumped into the road and cocked his weapon whilst pointing it at the car. It screeched to a halt. I was assured that the two occupants of the car did not need any extra fibre in their diet at that time.

I came round lying on my back with someone putting a First Field Dressing on the right side of my head. An RAF helicopter from Bessbrook was hovering over the top of us shining a bright searchlight. I could feel the downdraft and smell the distinct aroma of aviation fuel. The Section Commander waved off the helicopter as it was too dangerous to land because of nearby telephone wires. The Saracen Ambulance from our location was deployed at the same time as the helicopter and arrived shortly after it had been waved off. Our Section 2i/c Lance Corporal Paul Paisey was driving it. Paul was a big no-nonsense Junior NCO who punched first and asked questions later. I could hear the Claxton Horns wailing as he approached our location, he got out of the 'Can' with Cpl Bob Buckland, the Company RMA (Regimental Medical Assistant). Bob assessed my injuries as Paul shook my hand and thanked me profusely. "Cheers Harry mate! I got to use my blue light, horns and everything. You're a fucking star mate!"

"Glad I could help Paul," I mumbled.

In every location in NI, each Coy produced a list of all soldiers in that location and allocated each of them a death number. Each Arm was given a different colour code, the RCT's was blue and my number was nine. The number was put on a piece of Dynotape and stuck on the soldier's dog tags. In the event of a soldier being killed the death number could be given over the radio to identify him. Soldiers' names were never, but never, transmitted over the air. The section on the ground sent in a report that one of their 'Playtime' was down and they would require a replacement. HQ kept asking for confirmation of who was injured and the only way they could do that was by sending "Playtime Blue Nine is down". When the lads in the RCT accommodation were told to get a replacement out on the ground to replace Blue Nine, one of the lads checked the list on the wall and said, "Fuck me! Harry's dead!"

Paul and Bob took me to the Medical Centre at Bessbrook where an RAMC doctor sewed my very badly lacerated ear back onto my head. The doctor arranged for me to be taken back to Newry to collect my kit before I was taken to Ballykinler to recuperate for a couple of weeks. Ballykinler was a large Base Camp where our Troop HQ was co-located with 1st Battalion of the Black Watch Regiment, who were on a two-year tour of the Province.

When I walked into the RCT accommodation back in Newry the lads were very surprised to see me, as they thought I had been killed. They said my ear looked like it had been put through a meat grinder and my hair was all matted with dry blood. I went to my locker that I shared with two other blokes and all my kit was missing, even my unopened Christmas present that my wife had sent me was missing. They told me that as they thought I was dead they would help themselves to any good kit I may have had in my locker. Driver Morgan was wearing my new slippers (they were my unopened Christmas present) and complained, "I suppose you'll want these back then!"

My wife was about seven months pregnant with our son at the time of this accident and the Orderly Officer back in 10

Regiment called at our flat in Oerlinghausen to let her know what had happened. When a soldier is on an operational tour the last thing any army wife wants to see is the Orderly Officer knocking on your door. He won't be calling to check your electricity meter reading that is for sure. He told my wife "Look, it's nothing to worry about, old girl. It's nothing warlike. He's only had his head run over by a car. It's not as if he has been shot or blown up by a bomb or anything."

Someone from the Ministry of Defence phoned my dad, who was on duty in the Hospital Wing of Wormwood Scrubs at the time and said "Ah! Mr Clacy, it's about your son who is serving with the British Army in Northern Ireland, it is with deepest regret we have to tell you ... Hello ... Mr Clacy? Are you still there...?" He was still there, but lying on the floor after fainting. I stayed at Ballykinler for a couple of weeks until my ear had healed and my head shrunk back to its normal size and I could start wearing a driving helmet again.

After a week I started doing patrols with the Black Watch in Land Rovers. We would patrol up and down the minor roads that led to border crossing points into Southern Ireland. On one particular patrol we were out in two short-wheelbase Makralon Land Rovers at about 0200 hours; the other Land Rover was driven by one of the Black Watch's own MT drivers. We parked up in the middle of the road, setting up a VCP just over the rise in the road, so any approaching car would not be able to see us until they had come over the rise and into our checkpoint. They would not have the chance to stop, turn around and escape. We put out small red and white road signs that stated, *Army checkpoint. Turn off your headlights* at the side of the road, about 25 meters away from the VCP.

I was driving the rear Land Rover and when the front vehicle put on his four way flashers and pulled into the centre of the road I knew the Section Commander was setting up the VCP. It was pitch black as we were in the middle of the countryside and the only light was coming from the moon and stars. All the Black Jocks jumped out of my Land Rover and headed towards the other one that was carrying the Norwegian Container filled with hot sweet tea. I was left to guard the rear of our VCP on my own as they got themselves a hot brew.

It was such a narrow road that two cars would have to slow down to pass each other. There were knee-high embankments on both sides of the road with thin, weak hedges on the top of them.

I stood there for about ten minutes and started to shiver because it was a cold, damp night. I could see the headlights of a car approaching our VCP on the other side of the rise. As it came over the rise I was temporarily blinded by its headlights. The car stopped about 15 meters from where I was standing at the back of my Land Rover and kept its headlights on. I took out my torch and waved it at the windscreen of the car and shouted, "TURN OFF YOUR HEADLIGHTS!" Nothing happened for what seemed like a couple of minutes so I shouted again, "TURN OFF YOUR FUCKING HEADLIGHTS!"

At this point the headlights on the car were switched off and I could see a silhouette outline of the car. Its passenger door was open and a terrorist with an M16 rifle had climbed out, shut the door and dived into the ditch on the other side of the hedge. I couldn't believe what I was seeing. I cocked my SLR, took off the safety catch and pointed it at the guy who was just about to jump into the ditch and start shooting at me. To this very day I don't know why I didn't shoot him. Maybe I bottled it. Maybe something in the back of my mind was telling me something was not right.

One thing was for sure; I was very scared.

I must have shouted for the rest of the section because the next thing I remember they were all standing around me, asking what was happening. I burbled what had happened and a private from the section charged at the hedge, jumped over it and down into the ditch, after which we could hear the sounds of a face being rearranged by a very excited five-foot five-inch Caledonian psychopath. We dragged a semi-conscious body out of the ditch. He was wearing British Army Combat clothing. He was, in fact, a member of their own patrol.

When we pulled up to set up the VCP I thought everyone had gone to the front Land Rover to get a brew. I hadn't realised someone had dived into the hedge to cover me whilst I was stopping and searching vehicles. As the car approached and kept his headlights on, the sentry in the ditch jumped out, opened the passenger door and said, “Turn your lights off, now!” It was then that I saw him and the outline of the car as he shut the door and jumped through the hedge and back into the ditch. I now realise fear can make your brain wrongly interpret what you are seeing. He was a soldier, not a terrorist, and he was carrying an SLR not an M16 rifle. In films and TV programmes the viewer understands what is happening to all the protagonists as it is happening. The reality of being in a dangerous situation is very different, as this incident illustrates. It was lucky for both of us that I didn’t shoot, regardless of the reason why.

I returned to the location in Newry when my head had shrunk back to its normal size and I no longer looked like John Merrick. There was only about three weeks of the tour left before 10 Regiment returned to West Germany. When I got back in the RCT accommodation Paul Paisey told me that a huge rat he called ‘Seamus’ kept coming through the broken window in our room. The foot of Paul’s bed came level with the window. Outside the window was nothing but a large flat roof that was about 30 foot by 20 foot, so he had no idea where the rat was coming from. Paul got a rat-trap from the CQMS Stores and loaded it with a piece of Cheddar cheese. I did get to see the rat as I was nodding off one moonlit-night. The lights in the room were switched off and I was sleeping on the top bunk against the wall opposite the window when I heard some scratching noises. The rat was a big bastard and it came through the broken window and started running up and down the windowsill. He ate the cheese off the trap without setting it off, had a quick piss and a shit and fucked off to look for something else to eat.

He came back a few nights later and Paul had set the trap so it would be set off if the rat even farted in its general direction. Paul was in his bed and saw the rat as it approached the trap. It walked over the trap and set it off, but instead of having its neck snapped it was catapulted into the air in the direction of Paul. There was a flurry of activity as blankets, sheets and pillows flew all over the place and Paul screamed like a soprano with her arse on fire. We all got out of bed and chased it around the room until Paul killed it with the heel of one of his DMS boots. Paul picked up the flat corpse and threw it out of the broken window, shouting "AND FUCKING WELL STAY OUT!"

I was to see another rat, but this time it was in a VCP on the Dublin road coming from Southern Ireland and heading for Belfast. It was a Boom Town Rat by the name of Bob Geldof. He had just done a gig in the town of Dundalk in Southern Ireland and was travelling in a large, dark Transit van with 'The Boom Town Rats' painted on the side of the van and in white letters on the green plastic sunshade across the windscreen.

It was about 0200 hours and torrential rain was making our stag on duty a complete misery. I was sitting in the back of the 'Can' with the clipboard, taking down the details of drivers who came through the VCP, a cushy job when it is pissing it down with rain. The Patrol Commander was Corporal Brain of 2 RGJ. He was summoned by the Rifleman who was dealing with the driver of the Transit Van and from whom he was getting a lot of verbal diarrhoea. The occupants had all been asked to provide some form of identification and asked where they had come from and where they were heading. It was at this point the future 'Sir' Bob started mouthing it off.

"Were fucking musicians for Chroist's fucking sake. What have you fucking stopped us for? Do we look like fucking terrorists? Why don't you all fuck off back to fucking England and fucking leave us fucking alone you fucking idiots … for fuck's sake!"

Corporal Brain told the future 'Sir' Bob that we had a job to do trying to stop the terrorism in Northern Ireland and that if he would just be civil and assist us in our assignment he could continue on his journey very quickly. The future 'Sir' Bob couldn't leave it alone, though. He went on and on and on with the most abusive language that made even some of the Riflemen blush. Corporal Brain eventually snapped and ordered all the occupants out of the van and made them empty their electrical equipment out of the cargo area of the van in the pouring rain.

After searching the van we mounted up ready to move location and Corporal Brain shouted to the future 'Sir' Bob, "Thank you for your help Sir. I do hope you have a safe journey home."

9. Ups and Downs

The Squadron handed over to the incoming RCT unit and returned to Bielefeld for four weeks leave. My wife was about eight months pregnant at the time and was told she had some complications that would mean strict bed rest in hospital for the next 4–6 weeks. I therefore ended up running the flat, cooking, cleaning, shopping and washing for Matt, Naomi and myself. It was a sharp learning curve for a young man of 20 years old who was only used to looking after himself. I enjoyed the challenge to a degree but realised exactly how hard it is to run a family home on your own, especially when two young children are involved. The rest of the army wives in our block of flats were a tremendous help and clucked around me like a brood of mother hens. Every Sunday the three of us were invited to a different flat for a huge roast dinner.

I tried to get down to BMH (British Military Hospital) Rinteln to visit Ronnie with Matt and Naomi at least three times a week, but as I had to rely on welfare transport or borrowing a friend's car, it really was quite difficult. Ronnie was usually in a mood when we got there and always had something to complain about. She kept moaning to the Hospital staff that she wanted to go home as she knew there was nothing wrong with her. I hadn't realised she had a license to practice medicine. Ronnie always had an opinion on everything and it was always the right one. The Doctors in BMH Rinteln eventually got so fed up with her that they let her come home on Friday for the weekend as long as she continued with strict bed rest.

In the early hours of the Sunday morning Ronnie woke me up saying she was bleeding and suffering from abdominal pain. Doctors one, Ronnie Nil. I got dressed and ran round to 'The Battleship' – a large grey elongated block of flats where Toddy Doran lived. He was an RAMC Medic Full Screw who worked in the Medical Centre in Ripon Barracks. He had a telephone in his flat and told his wife to phone the Medical Centre and ask for an ambulance to be sent to my flat as soon as possible. We ran back to my place and he could see that the sheets on the bed were soaked in quite a lot of blood. He told me to get a couple of dining chairs.

'This is no time to organise a fucking dinner party', I thought, but as I came back to the bedroom with the chairs Toddy was reassuring Ronnie that everything was going to be OK and not to worry. He took one of the chairs and told me to lift up the end of the bed; we did this and placed the chairs under it so the bed was propped up at an angle. Ronnie's legs were now in an elevated position and hopefully arresting the bleeding with the help of a sanitary towel that Toddy sent me to find. I felt useless but Toddy was so calm and confident, he took complete control and commanded everything. I was so glad that he was there.

The ambulance came and we loaded Ronnie inside and took her to the Medical Centre in Ripon Barracks where the Duty Medical Officer sent us straight to the local Krankenhaus. He said she needed to get to a hospital as quickly as possible.

A grey-haired and petite female German doctor called Dr Frau Hempfing met us in the foyer of the Krankenhaus wearing a long, white doctor's coat. She had been informed we were coming by the Duty Medical officer and had obviously been given his diagnosis. Ronnie was laid on an army stretcher in the Krankenhaus foyer as the doctor placed a square microphone on her tummy and we all listened for the baby's heartbeat. Nothing. She placed it on another part after having again prodded Ronnie's tummy and we listened for even the slightest sign of a heartbeat. Nothing. The doctor tried at least a dozen times to find a heartbeat but to no avail.

"I am so sorry Frau Clacy but your baby is dead," she said. "I am afraid we will have to operate on you tonight to terminate this pregnancy."

Ronnie was sobbing and I was trying to hold myself together as the army medic put his hand on my shoulder and said "Sorry mate." Ronnie pleaded with the doctor to try one more time. She tried a couple more times and eventually found the faintest of heartbeats.

"Mein Gott!" she exclaimed. "Get Frau Clacy up on to a ward immediately!"

I lost control and started to sob. There was not a dry eye in the house. Even the army medic was wiping his eyes.

Ronnie stayed in the Krankenhaus for the rest of her pregnancy and gave birth to our son Daniel on 22 June 1978. We named him Daniel after the biblical story of Daniel who got out alive from the lion's den.

I did a TTF and POD Operators course in the regiment. This Course taught Drivers how to drive and operate fuel tankers that were used to refuel units in the field. The largest tanker we had in 10 Regiment was the Foden 22,500 litre, which was an absolute joy to drive, and the smallest was called a POD. This was a flatbed MK 4-tonner with two large fuel tanks bolted on the back, one tank for petrol and the other for diesel. These were used as a mobile petrol station for the unit's own vehicles and the Fodens were used to re-supply the PODs. Cyril Tickle, my Saracen driving instructor, was one of the instructors on the course. We had to do some driver training but the majority of the course involved Safety Regulations and the mechanics of using the pumps and other equipment. The first thing a driver had to do after parking up was put an earth line in the ground. This was similar to a large metal tent peg and was attached to the tanker with a long insulated wire cable. This was put into the ground in case the tanker was hit by an electrical storm and it also drained any built up static electricity from the vehicle. All the tools for the TTFs and PODs were all specially made non-spark type.

I passed the course and joined A Troop 36 Squadron TTF and POD Detachment and adapted to my new role in the Regiment. One of the main differences on Exercise was that all TTF and POD drivers were not allowed to sleep in their vehicles, because of the obvious fire and fumes hazard. We were also not allowed to scrim up (camouflage) the tankers, as anyone who has scrimmed up a fully loaded 10-tonner with a trailer will understand. Scrim nets are made out of a tough green string with green and brown plastic camouflage squares tied on to it. These bloody things snagged on every part of the wagon and local flora that you didn't want it to snag on, but would not stay attached to any part of the wagon or local flora you wanted it to stay attached to. None of the scrim nets should be touching the vehicle after it has been put on, large wooden poles were used to make it into a camouflage garage. All scrimming up had to be done immediately on entering your hide in a wood (except at night when you would only have to apply your hessian skirt and cab cover, you would still have to fully scrim up before first light though). This had to be done whilst wearing full webbing and carrying your personal weapon, both of which loved to attach themselves to any scrim net you went within arm's length of. By the time your wagon was fully scrimmed up you would be soaked in sweat and bitten to death by insects in the summer. To add to your misery and frustration you would have your Troop Sergeant shouting and screaming at you to "GET A FUCKING GRIP! THERE COULD BE RUSSIAN MIG FIGHTER BOMBERS ON THEIR WAY TO STICK AN AIR TO GROUND MISSILE UP YOUR FUCKING ARSE!" That would have been a joy in comparison to having your eardrums burst by a gobby Sergeant.

One of the SSMs in 10 Regt used to inspect all his Drivers scrimming up and completed it with, "I am the wind! Whoooooooo." He would then launch himself at your scrim nets with such speed and weight it would usually collapse. He would then walk off saying "Sort it out gnome, I'll be back in 10 minutes."

We in the TTF and POD section did not have to put up with all this crap anymore. We also had our own tents as we could not sleep in the vehicles and were therefore issued with army camp beds. Pure luxury compared to sleeping on a 10-tonner engine-cover.

On my first Exercise with the TTF Section we had to be located near to main roads, as the tankers could not be parked on soft ground. About 20 meters away from our tent was a 12 by 12 (all tentage in the British Army is referred to by its size in feet) tent that was used to cover six chemical bucket toilets.

This tent was sited about 15 meters from a busy main road and at the end of the Exercise we were told to take down all tentage and pack it away on the G1098 wagon. The 12 by 12 was packed away and two rows of chemical toilets were left in full view of the German public as they drove past.

I arrived back at our location after filling up a TTF at Warendorf, the British military fuel supply depot for West Germany. The weather was overcast and spitting with rain, the wind was blowing quite hard as I entered our location in the TTF and I noticed the two rows of chemical toilets. On one of them was our Section Commander called Jed, he had his Combat trousers round his ankles and was having a crap whilst reading a newspaper that was flapping about in the wind. He took the time to wave at the cars that tooted at him as they drove past, laughing at his big spotty arse.

I had been recommended for promotion to Lance Corporal by my Troop Staff Sergeant Clive Symonds, a tall, thin dark haired man with a sense of humour that was second to none. He wore a pair of black-rimmed glasses that he had borrowed from Brains in *Thunderbirds*. He warned me off for OC's Orders one day and told me to bring in my best boots; he said the OC wanted to interview me about my drop in standards since my recommendation for promotion. Staff Symonds said, "If you want to get on in the RCT, Driver Clacy, you had better listen to what he has to say. He had great hopes for you but feels you have let yourself down recently".

I couldn't think of what I had done wrong but I said "OK Staff". The following day I reported to the Chief Clerk at 0900 hours in heavily-starched working dress and highly-bulled best boots. There were five other Drivers waiting for interviews; some were there on charges for various misdemeanours. I was third to be marched in and noticed that the previous two had looked pretty pissed off when they had been marched out by the SSM. The SSM marched me into the OC's office and halted me in front of his desk.

I saluted and very nervously said, "Good morning Sir".

The OC looked very stern. "Good morning Driver Clacy, do you know why I have ordered you to come and see me this morning?" he asked.

"Yes Sir," I replied.

"Good, then tell me why you are here Driver Clacy," said the OC.

"I don't know Sir," I stupidly replied.

The OC and SSM both started to laugh and shake their heads. The OC opened his right hand drawer and took out a Lance Corporal tape and placed it on the desk in front of him. "Manning and Records have selected you to be promoted to Lance Corporal, though God knows why after that display of your decisiveness". He told me that he knew I was nervous about this interview but that he and Staff Symonds had been very impressed with me over the last year or so. He reminded me that this was the hardest promotion to win and the easiest to lose. I should go away and build on the good work I had started and he would be scrutinising my conduct very closely. I thanked him, saluted, about-turned and the SSM marched me out on a cloud of air.

I reported back to the Troop Office and was met by Staff Symonds, who had a big grin on his face as he shook my hand, "Congratulations Corporal Clacy, you're now on the bottom rung, make sure you don't let me down by fucking falling off it!"

"I won't Staff," I said. Staff Symonds had an arm brassard with a Lance Corporal tape on it that I could wear until all my uniforms were tailored. I sat on the floor by the Troop Office door and took off my best boots and put on my working boots. The bully who had bayoneted the soldier on our JLR Passing Out Parade came out of B Troop office, noticed the brassard and sneered as he said "Fucking hell! They're giving tapes away to anyone these days." Staff Symonds came out from behind the door and said, "No they fucking aren't. You have to earn promotion and respect, something you are never likely to achieve! If you ever talk to one of my NCOs like that again I will make your fucking life even more miserable than it is now! GET OUT OF MY SIGHT YOU HORRIBLE LITTLE MAN!"

"Yes Staff, sorry Staff" he quivered. Staff Symonds had a great sense of humour but was absolutely fearsome when annoyed. "You're going to get a lot of shit like this over the next few weeks until things settle down," he advised me.

Staff Symonds was eventually promoted to SSM of 36 Squadron and on a Working Parade one morning he replaced all Officers and NCOs with Drivers and let them run the Squadron for the day. It was a brilliant morale-building Exercise and he played the part of an indolent, witless Driver superbly.

As a newly-promoted Junior NCO I was moved into a 36 Squadron MT Corporal job. This involved checking all the documentation and monitoring the servicing schedules for the vehicles in the Squadron. Military vehicles are serviced at regular intervals to ensure they are kept in a reliable and safe condition. Each vehicle has a work ticket in a green denim folder and this is filled in every time a Driver takes a vehicle out on a detail or exercise. The date and timings of the journey, destination and start and finish milometer readings are always filled in. The folder also contained a copy of Military Drivers Standing Orders, an FMT 3 (accident report form), a copy of BFG (British Forces Germany) Highway Code, contact numbers in the event of a breakdown as well as the keys for the vehicle and any padlocks. My job was to check the work tickets were correctly maintained and when a vehicle reached a certain mileage make sure it was put in for the relevant servicing schedule in our Squadron servicing bay. It was the second most horrendously boring job in the RCT. I had already done the first, which was working in the Squadron servicing bay and carrying out the actual servicing schedules. Changing the oil in an axle differential or greasing up some other part of the underside of a 10-tonner had already nearly bored me to death.

I had been a Lance Corporal for about two weeks when I started to realise how difficult it was to keep everyone happy as a Junior NCO. I went on the Squadron vehicle park one day to tell a Driver to take his wagon to the servicing bay for its due servicing. The usual playful banter started and I was held down on the floor while the lads gave me a pretend beating. One of the Troop Sergeants from 9 Squadron was walking past and started to give us all a bollocking for messing about.

He turned to me and said, "Start behaving like a fucking NCO. You are not one of the lads any more. We expect better than this from Junior NCOs!"

I was embarrassed and felt lower than a snakes belly at the bottom of the Grand Canyon. The next time I saw some lads clowning around I gave them a balling out and they had a go at me about my rank going to my head.

"You used to be a good lad, Harry, but now you think you're better than us because you've got a bit of bird shit on your arm".

It was a difficult time for me and, I suppose, for every other Lance Corporal in the world. You have to work through this period and hopefully earn the respect and trust of the guys you are there to command.

Several months later I started to feel very tired in the evenings, in fact I fell asleep at someone's flat during a party even though music was blaring and people were dancing around the chair I had fallen asleep in. They must have assumed I was pissed and had passed out; the fact of the matter was I had only had a couple of Herforder Pils beers. I got up in the mornings and felt exhausted. I used to get a lift into work with my mate Cyril Tickle and he once found me asleep resting my head on the wing of his car whilst I sat on the kerb waiting for him to come out of his flat. I also noticed that I had to go for a piss more than usual and I was thirsty all the time. I used to carry a 1-litre bottle of water to quench my thirst on the 20-minute journey from Oerlinghausen to Catterick Barracks every morning. Ronnie was quite concerned as I was falling asleep talking to people who visited us during the evenings.

I reported sick to the retired Lieutenant Colonel Medical Officer in Ripon Barracks, and gave him the following signs and symptoms:

a. Extreme thirst (and not just for beer).

b. Lethargy in excess of even the laziest British Soldier.

c. Severe weight loss (I had dropped from 11 ½ stone to 8 stone).

d. Urine output to extreme (soldiers usually take the piss, not give it).

e. Unbearable itch on my foreskin (this turned out to be thrush).

The first thing the MO asked me was, "Have you had a sexual experience with a German woman of loose morals?"

When I replied "No Sir" I half expected him to say, "You should try it, it's awfully good fun!" He seemed disappointed that he had to rule out venereal disease as the cause of my symptoms. He gave me a glucose-based tonic to improve my appetite and hopefully gain some weight.

I was back out on Exercise the following week, driving a TTF 22500 litre Tanker filled up to the brim with AVTUR (Aviation Fuel for helicopters). AVTUR will explode if you look at it the wrong way. I was still very tired and finding it difficult to stay awake. The glucose-based tonic seemed to make me feel even more tired. Before I went on the Exercise a mate who lived near me in Oerlinghausen, Driver 'Robbo' Robinson, spoke to me about what he thought was medically wrong with me.

"I think you've got diabetes, mate", he said. He wasn't sure of the details about diabetes but seemed to think it involved me having too much sugar in my blood. I shrugged off his comments. What would he know about anything medical, he was only a Driver in the RCT.

On a Sunday afternoon during the Exercise, after I had refuelled at Warendorf, I called into my flat in Oerlinghausen to fill up my water bottles and have a cup of tea with the family. I left the TTF parked out the front of the block of flats. Matthew was about 9 years old at the time and seemed to be very impressed that his dad was driving this monster of a truck and had come home with a rifle. He was disappointed that I wouldn't let him take it out to play with his friends.

Ronnie had been round to the Families' Medical Centre in the Battleship block earlier in the week to ask the nurse for some advice about my tiredness. She gave Ronnie a urine sample bottle and asked her to bring it in for testing after I had filled it; I gave her the sample that she would take in on the Monday morning for testing. I then got back in the TTF and returned to my unit location in the field and continued with the Exercise.

First thing on Monday morning, after dropping the kids off at school, Ronnie called into the Medical Centre and gave the sample to the nurse, who stuck a test strip in the urine and checked it against the guide. The sugar level was at 2% on the scale and the ketones were dangerously high. The nurse told Ronnie that she believed I was diabetic and because I had been like this for so long I could go into a coma at some stage.

Robbo One, Royal Army Medical Corps Nil.

"Where is your husband at the moment Mrs Clacy?" asked the nurse.

"On Exercise driving a massive tanker fully loaded with aviation fuel," said Ronnie.

I was out on the road at the time the Squadron CP was informed of my medical dilemma. They had RMP patrols driving up and down the MSRs looking for me and my potential petrol bomb. When I eventually arrived at the Squadron Hide it was about midnight. I was taken to the CP and told I had to report straight to the Medical Centre in Ripon Barracks. The OCs Driver was to take me straight there and under no circumstances was I to do any further driving. We arrived at Ripon Barracks at about 0300 hours and the Duty Medic told me the MO was in bed and I would have to report sick in the morning but make sure I ate plenty of sweet things until then.

After reporting sick in the morning I was taken to BMH Rinteln and admitted onto the Medical Ward, where they told me I had Type 1 diabetes, which mean's my pancreas was not producing any insulin at all. They started me on an insulin regime to get my blood sugars under control. The problem with diabetics is that their pancreas does not produce enough of the hormone insulin that controls the absorption of sugars by the body. Much of the carbohydrate in food is converted into glucose and insulin enables most body cells (primarily muscle and fat) to absorb glucose from the blood and use it for energy. A lack of insulin causes the liver to turn fat into ketone particles (a fuel mainly used for the brain).

That explained my ketoacidosis, lethargy, weight loss and lack of concentration. Did you get all that? Good.

After a couple of days I started to feel a lot better and the thrush cleared up quickly after I had applied some Canesten cream. At its worst stage I had rubbed my foreskin red raw and it was very painful, yet it still caused me so much discomfort because it still itched whilst remaining painful. It was embarrassing on Exercise as my Troop Sergeant accused me of having a wank whilst on Stand To. I explained I was just having a good scratch of my foreskin as I had an infection and offered to show him to prove it. He declined the invitation.

After a week of having insulin injections, blood tests and 4 times daily urine checks the Consultant Medical Officer told me I had to start injecting myself because I was going to have to do it for the rest of my life. I was very nervous on the morning I was to start this. I reported to the treatment room and sat next to an 8-year-old child who drew up insulin in a glass syringe, wiped his leg with an alcohol swab and injected the insulin without blinking an eyelid. I was very impressed and told him so.

"This is my first time," I said.

He told me not to worry about it because "It's a piece of piss. Do you want me to talk you through it?" Some Forces children appear to have an abundance of confidence. I bet his dad was a Sergeant Major.

I also had to start learning about the value of carbohydrates in certain food categories and how to balance that with the amount of insulin I was taking. In the late 1970s the main insulins were extracted from pork and beef and had varying strengths; some were long acting and others slow acting. They all came in 20, 40, 60 and 100 strength vials. If you had to take 10 units of Actrapid 20, you could use Actrapid 40 and only draw up 5 units. It involved using a small mathematical equation but you had to make sure you were paying attention every time you drew up your insulin. I left hospital about six weeks after being admitted and only after they had put me through a deliberately-induced hypoglycaemic (low blood sugar) attack. This involved me having my insulin at lunchtime but not eating anything until I felt the effects of having a low blood sugar. When you start to feel hungry, weak, confused and your hands start to tremble it is time to get something to eat to stop your blood sugar falling. The mistake a lot of people make when treating a hypoglycaemic semi-conscious diabetic is that they believe "He's diabetic and needs his medicine." They then inject insulin that will lower his blood sugar even more and will eventually put the patient into a coma and could cause a whole load of other problems. If you give a hypoglycaemic diabetic a glass of full fat milk and a couple of digestive biscuits they will become *compos mentis*[1] in no time at all. This can only be done if they are conscious; if semi-conscious it is possible to rub some form of dextrose gel on the patient's gums and await some trained medical assistance.

Good grief, I sound like a training manual.

The Consultant Medical Officer came to see me before I was discharged from the hospital and informed me that:

a. I was of no further use to the Army and would probably be discharged from the Forces as soon as I was posted back to the UK.

b. The Army could not be held to account for this happening to me so I could forget about any chance of obtaining compensation.

c. DVLA would revoke my HGV licenses immediately as I was now going to be a liability when in charge of any motor vehicle.

d. I had served less than 12 years and would not be getting a gratuity or pension for the time I had served in the Army.

After leaving the Army in 1993 I was awarded a War Pension. It was deemed too much of a coincidence from my head injury in Newry and the signs and symptoms of diabetes starting.

---

[1] Latin for 'in control of one's mind.'

Things were not looking good for me. I was a married father of three young children, the army had no further use for me, I had no savings or trade behind me and was now an insulin-dependent diabetic...

1. Cyprus 1963 – A Crap Hat in the making.

2. Belfast 1976 – Protestant area.

3. Chris Lovett, 3 Para.

4. Inside Mulhouse Location with Kev Carter 1976.

5. JMQC Course 1978.
Author is in the rear rank, 4th from the right. Dave North also in rear rank, far left.

6. Me and my Pig – Belfast 1976.

7. Sandy Row Belfast 1976.

10. Tidworth

Manning and Records posted me back to 66 Squadron RCT in Jellelabad Barracks, Tidworth Garrison, near Salisbury. 66 Squadron was reformed as a new unit and adopted the Phoenix rising from the flames as its new unit plaque symbol. Quite a few of the lads from 10 Regiment had also come to make up the full complement of the new Squadron. It was good to see that Corporal Steve Bytner, a bull of a man with a bellowing voice to match, had taken over as the new Squadron RP (Regimental Police) NCO. Steve had won an MID (Mentioned in Despatches) award for gallantry on his previous tour of duty in NI with 10 Regiment. A stolen white Ford transit van driven by two men with probable IRA connections broke through a cordon and nearly hit an RUC policeman and a soldier, Steve jumped into his 'Pig' and blocked the van's escape route. In spite of their efforts to evade capture the men were captured and arrested.

Corporal Paul Paisey, who picked me up in the Saracen Ambulance in Newry after sustaining my head injury, was also posted in to 66 Squadron. It was a very uncertain and nervous time for me as I had no idea what was going to happen to me and my family, so to see some friendly albeit very tough faces was quite reassuring.

I was allocated a 3-bedroom Married Quarter in Kohat Close. The house was clean but damp and the decoration was in a very poor state; the paint in the sitting room was flaking off the walls. The EW (Estate Warden) who moved us into the Married Quarter told me there was no money available for decoration, but if I wanted to buy the paint and decorate the house using my own funds that would be alright. Bizarrely, he stated I would have to return it to its original state before I moved out. The windows were all single glazed and set in very old-fashioned metal window frames. During the winter all the curtains in the house were constantly moving because of the draughts coming through the gaps where the windows were buckled.

Wives were not allowed in the Married Quarter during the handover/takeover; I think this ruling was instigated to avoid the EWs having the shit beaten out of them by some very angry Army wives who felt the MQ did not meet their standards. The histrionics started as soon as Ronnie came in the house after the officials had departed. The open-mouthed look of horror as she held her head in her hands would not have looked out of place in a Charlie Chaplin film.

I reported to the Squadron and was interviewed by the OC Major Morrison. He told me I would be employed as the SSMs clerk, which involved minor admin jobs and a lot of running around doing nothing. I told him of my concerns for the future. He tried to reassure me that he would do everything within his powers to help my family and me. Major Morrison was single but was very aware of the needs and problems of his married soldiers. He personally visited the Squadron wives in the wives club and in the Married Quarters, a job normally carried out by the OC's wife. He was an absolute gentleman and a man of action; he would never do something tomorrow. "Come on, let's get this bloody thing sorted out" could have been his family motto.

I did the SSMs clerk job with a certain amount of bad grace as I wanted to be out on the vehicle park with the lads. I wanted to be out on the road driving a fucking big truck. That was what I had joined the Royal Corps of Transport for, not collecting the mail for the Orderly Room. The Chief Clerk was Staff Sergeant Healey and he was very helpful to me. He said if I re-traded as a clerk in the RCT I would possibly be able to carry on with my Army career. He arranged for me to go on the All Arms Clerk Course at Blackdown Barracks at Deepcut near Aldershot. I was doing quite well up to the third week of the course. My father was, at this time, stationed at an open prison near Devizes, about 40 minutes drive from Tidworth. He came to visit me and suggested I try and get into the Prison Service, as it was a well-paid job with a good pension scheme. I RTU'd (Return to Unit) myself off the course and reported to Staff Healey and told him of my intentions to try my luck in Civvy Street. He seemed disappointed by my decision and was probably annoyed as he and the OC had made such great efforts for my family and me to remain in the Army. To this very day I regret the fact that I let Staff and the OC down without so much as a 'kiss my arse'! Sorry guys.

I went for an interview and medical at HMP Winchester and as soon as I told the Prison Doctor I was diabetic he told me it was unlikely I would be accepted as a Prison officer.

"There are all sorts of problems with a diabetic serving in the Prison Service. I should know, because I am diabetic myself," he said.

"Well why the fuck did they give you a job then?" I replied.

Apparently, his case was an entirely different matter. He told me I would have to write to the Home Office for special dispensation. They wrote back to me and thanked me for my letter but in the politest words possible could I please fuck off at the high port. So I was back to square one, no job and no long-term career with a family to feed.

On one of my visits to my doctor at the Medical Centre in Tidworth I met our Squadron RMA (Regimental Medical Assistant), who was an RCT Lance Corporal. He told me he was posted back to West Germany and the Group Practice was looking for a replacement to look after the Squadron's Medical Documents and deal with Sick Parades, etc.

In Tidworth and in the early 1980s the Garrison consisted of, in no particular order (before you all start complaining about your Regiment being senior to someone else's):

1 Battalion Cheshire Regiment (Infantry)
Queens Royal Irish Hussars (Tank Regiment)
2 Battalion Royal Irish Rangers (Infantry)
3 Battalion Parachute Regiment (Infantry)
66 Squadron RCT
2 Battalion Royal Green Jackets (Infantry)
1 Battalion Light Infantry (Infantry, obviously)
17/21 Lancers (Cavalry- Donkey Wallopers)
22 Engineer Regiment (RE)
DMed (Defence Medical Equipment Depot - RAMC)
10 Field Workshops (REME)

CVD (Combined Vehicle Depot- RAOC)

Each of these units had their own Medical team working in the Group Practice in Tidworth. The infantry Battalions would have their own Medical Officer, RMA Sergeant, RMA Corporal, and about 4 Lance-Corporal or Private RMAs. All members of these medical teams were trained soldiers from their own Corps and Regiments and therefore wore their own Cap Badges. The only members of the team that were RAMC were the doctors. All the other units had a single RMA to deal with their own particular unit requirements. 66 Squadron's RMA was also responsible for 10 Field Workshop, DMed and the CVD documents and personnel when they reported sick.

I didn't want to be the SSM's clerk until the Army decided what they were going to do with me so I decided to take the job. My predecessor also told me that there were no Working Parades and I would be left to get on with my work without any interference from the Squadron. The Group Practice Manager was a WO2 Gooding RAMC, who looked like Danger Mouse's sidekick Penfold, a calm and quietly spoken man who took great pains to help me learn and settle into the job.

The RMA Corporal for 2 RGJ was Cpl Bob Buckland, the RMA who came to treat me when I received my head injury on the Dublin Road just outside Newry. He was a calm, big bloke and one of the older Corporals in the Battalion. He had read the book, seen the film and acted in the play on all aspects of Army Life. In Newry, when I went for a piss, I noticed blood coming out from under one of the cubicle doors. I looked underneath and saw a very pale-faced soldier slumped forward on the toilet. He had obviously slashed his wrists in an attempt to commit suicide. Bob's Medical room was situated next to the toilets; he used the room as a treatment room as well as his accommodation. I ran into his room and told him what I had seen. He grabbed a webbing First Aid bag and ran next door. The cubicle door was locked so Bob stepped back and stuck his size 12 DMS boot against it (John Wayne couldn't have done it better) and the cubicle door flew open. Unfortunately the bloke inside was leaning forward and the edge of the cubicle door put a dent in his forehead.

Bob had to stop his bleeding from the wrist and then treat him for a head injury.

Bob said to me, "It's never like this in the movies is it?"

I started to learn about the documentation of the FMed 4, which is a stout folder holding a soldier's personal medical history. It holds the records of vaccinations, blood group, eye and hearing tests, chest x-rays, colour perception, sensitivity to drugs and treatment cards that record any treatment he will have received during his military career. Fmed 4s were kept in a locked filing cabinet in alphabetical order and accompanied a soldier in a sealed envelope when he was admitted to hospital, sent on a Course or attended an Out-Patients Appointment. A soldier's PULHEEMS were also recorded on the Fmed 4, each letter referred to a different medical aspect of the soldier:

P Physical capacity
U Upper limbs
L Locomotion and lower limbs
H Hearing
E Eye (Right)
E Eye (Left)
M Mental capacity
S Emotional Stability

A soldier was examined on all of the above and graded between 1 and 4 on each facet when he joined the army, reached the age of 30 and above or received a severe injury. He was given a Pulheems Employment Standard, these determined where a soldier could serve in the battle area anywhere around the world:

FE Forward Everywhere
FT Forward Temperate
LE Lines of Communication Everywhere
LT Lines of Communication Temperate
BE Base Everywhere
BT Base Temperate
HO Home Only

HO UK Home Only UK/not British Army of the Rhine
HO UK NNI Home Only UK/ not Northern Ireland

After being diagnosed with diabetes I was given a Pulheems Employment Standard of P4 HO UK NNI. I was excused all physical activities but breathing and could only serve in the UK.

I also learned about soldiers' vaccinations: when they were given, which were required for different countries around the world and how to arrange a vaccination clinic for my unit. As my unit was quite small I did 66 Squadron's , DMed's, 10 Field Wksp's and CVD's all on the same clinic. I sent out a list of names for units to put on Part One Orders and notify when they should report to the Medical Centre for their jabs. These vaccination parades were usually done in the afternoon after the mayhem of Morning Sick Parade had calmed down.

Bob showed me how to organise and set up everything and said he would run the clinic for me so I could learn how things were done. I had a copy of each Unit Part One Orders to tick off the soldiers who attended and who didn't. I also had each soldier's FMed 4 and entered the details of their vaccination date and batch number on the vial as the jab was given. Bob showed me how to administer Polio, Tabt, Smallpox and Yellow Fever inoculations. After watching a couple of each he said "Right! Your turn now." It's always a very sharp learning curve in the Army. I was used to doing injections on myself but to do it on someone else was a different matter. The Polio inoculation was the easiest as it just involved putting three small drops of the inoculation onto the patient's tongue from a small rubber vial. I asked what happened to the box of sugar cubes used for administering the foul tasting Polio.

"That's in our tea room," said Bob.

The doctor I worked for was Lt Col (Retd) O'Dwyer, a bad-tempered Irishman who often used to enjoy extended liquid lunch breaks in the Officers Mess. He used to get very annoyed if you tried to squeeze another patient in to see him in the afternoon, especially if they had reported 'Special Sick'.

"Go and find out why he didn't come on this morning's Sick Parade," was his usual cry.

After speaking to the patient I would tell him, "He wasn't feeling that bad this morning, so he decided to wait and see if he was going to be alright."

"For God's sake, am I the only doctor working this afternoon? Jesus H Christ! Alright, bring him in and I'll have a look at him!"

Lt Col O'Dwyer: "What is the matter with you young man?"

Patient: "I have stomach pains and I feel sick sir".

Lt Col O'Dwyer: "Why didn't you come in on Sick Parade this morning?"

Patient: "I didn't feel too bad this morning sir and decided to see if I felt better later on. My SSM says he doesn't like the look of me and told me to come and see you sir."

Lt Col O'Dwyer: "You can report back to your SSM and tell him that I think you are ugly too but why does he need me to confirm it."

Lt Col O'Dwyer would always see any extra patients but we would have to go through a similar charade every time before he would eventually agree to the appointment.

Morning Sick Parades were usually absolute mayhem. Soldiers from each Company or Squadron had to report to their respective CSM or SSM and explain why they wanted to report sick. The Orderly Room Clerk would then list all the names of the soldiers reporting sick on an Fmed (Form Medical) 566 and the SSM would sign the bottom of the form. If you were reporting 'Special Sick' it was written in red ink. The senior soldier amongst the sick, lame and lazy would then march them all down to the Medical Centre and hand the Fmed 566 to their unit RMAs.

We would then get out their Fmed 4s, examine and treat those we could deal with and prepare those that were going in to see the doctor. We might have to take and record TPRs (Temperature, Pulse and Respiration) on the treatment cards in the soldiers Fmed 4, test urine samples, take blood pressures and generally examine the patient for whatever his complaint was. The Fmed 4s were then put on the doctor's desk and patients lined up outside his surgery, after the doctor had finished he would send the patient to the pharmacy with a prescription or back to the treatment room for the RMAs to carry out the treatment necessary. Strapping up sprained ankles, syringing wax out of ears and applying medicaments and dressings were all the usual day-to-day chores. Next to the patients name on the Fmed 566 was noted the disposal of that particular soldier and the number of days that were relevant:

A4 = Attend at the Medical Centre in 4 days time.
B2 = Light Duties for 2 days.
C7 = Bedded down for 7 days.
M&D = Medicine and Duties
Hosp = Admitted to hospital.

The last soldier out of the doctor's surgery would take the Fmed 566, signed by the doctor, back to the unit so they would know the disposal of each soldier.

By the time I went on my RMA Course at the RAMC Depot at Ash Vale near Aldershot I had become adept at dealing with Sick Parades, taking blood pressures, giving vaccinations and a whole host of other medical missions. The RMAs and civilian nurses who worked in the Group Practice taught all these things to me. The RMA Course was exactly the same Course that was run for the Medical Assistants, our opposite numbers in the RAMC. These days they are called Combat Medical Technicians and, as in my time, they are highly trained and capable lifesavers and sustainers. There was a whole host of things to learn on the course, ranging from anatomy and physiology to the Clinical Phase, where you had to set up a tracheotomy trolley under sterile conditions. On the test day if you rubbed your face during the set-up procedure, you would be failed for cross contamination. The standard expected by the instructors and testing staff was very high.

I had found a new job and trade in the world of medicine and I loved it more than driving trucks. I passed the Course and couldn't wait to get back to work in the Group Practice. All the RMAs wore a brassard on their left arm that held pens, pencils, a pair of surgical scissors and a pair of Spencer Wells forceps. The scissors were used to cut dressings and clothing when dealing with casualties and the Spencer Wells forceps used when suturing open wounds. I got myself an old brassard and kitted it out with the appropriate stationery and surgical equipment. I now felt like one of the gang.

WO2 Gooding left the Group Practice for pastures new and was replaced by WO2 Bernie Wray RAMC who came to us from 22 SAS Regiment. He had been a Patrol Medic whilst serving in the Regiment. He was a wiry, balding, fair haired man who, although quietly spoken, could be extremely sarcastic and was the most confident man I think I had met up to that point in my life. He always went for a 10 mile run at lunchtime and I don't think I ever saw him eat anything.

He started giving lectures in the afternoons for all the RMAs, these were held in his office at least three times a week and he called them 'Matters Medical'. The lectures covered anything and everything medical; subjects ranged from Venereal Disease to setting up and administering Intravenous Infusions (drips). After a couple of weeks instructing us he wrapped up a lecture one afternoon with a little announcement.

"I am sure you are all sick to death of hearing the sound of my voice so Lance Corporal Shaw (Cheshire Regiment) will give a lecture on Friday afternoon on Chemical Burns and the treatment thereof. If you need any help or advice on your lecture come and see me and I will be more than glad to help. Any questions? No … Good. Everyone will at some stage have to give a lecture of my choosing, lecturing will increase your learning power."

I never got tired of hearing Bernie Wray's lectures. He had an endless amount of fascinating and funny stories, but I found the apprehension of arranging and giving a lecture myself quite addictive. He was also right about our learning power. Having to read up on a subject you knew nothing about previously and then imparting that knowledge to others was a great way to learn. Sadly, Bernie Wray was run over by a truck and killed whilst taking part in a marathon run in Kenya. I learned so much from him and he also gave me the bug for lecturing, something that I would excel at in 'Matters Medical' and NBC (Nuclear Biological and Chemical Warfare) later in my career.

The RMAs in the Group Practice never did any duties within their own units, so we never stagged on guard outside our unit Guardrooms. We had to do duties that were run by Bernie Wray; these involved running evening clinics for all service families and soldiers from 1800 hours to 1900 hours in the Group Practice with the Duty MO and civilian nurses. After locking up when the evening clinic was finished the Duty RMA and MO moved down to the MRS (Medical Reception Station), which was similar to a mini hospital. It had a 12 bed ward with a couple of isolation bunks and a small kitchen. All emergency cover for the whole Garrison was covered from the MRS at night and over the entire weekend. The MRS was administered by a mixture of QARANC (Queen Alexandra's Royal Army Nursing Corps), RAMC and Civilian Staff. Two old white Bedford Ambulances provided emergency transport to either Salisbury infirmary or RAF Wroughton Hospital. Weekend duties ran from 0800 hours to 0800 hours the following day, any emergency call outs were dealt with by either the RAMC or RMA duty medic.

I enjoyed the drama of an emergency call-out to the Married Quarter area. The MRS telephone number was published in the Garrison Families Guide and seemed to be the first number anyone called before considering 999.

I was duty RMA one Sunday and was dispatched with Alex the Civilian Ambulance Driver to pick up an army wife in Perham Down who had severe abdominal pain. When we arrived at the Married Quarter we were met at the front door by the patient's friend. She urged us into the sitting room as she felt her friend was at death's door. The patient was lying on the settee with her knees drawn up and looked very pale. She appeared to be in a lot of pain. She was a short, slightly tubby woman, who was wearing a pair of jeans that must have belonged to a woman two stone lighter. The television was on and they had been watching the Sunday afternoon film whilst stuffing their faces with peanuts, crisps and glasses of Ginger Beer. She told me the pain had started about three hours previously. She wasn't pregnant and didn't have any stomach or bowel problems that she knew of. She clearly hadn't strained herself through over exercising, so I thought we had better get her to the MRS so the Doc could have a look at her. Alex got the chair lift device out of the ambulance, as she felt she could not walk out to the ambulance.

By the time we arrived back at the MRS there were a mixture of soldiers, wives and children in the Waiting Room outside the Treatment Room to see the Doc with the usual minor cough and cold ailments that really could have waited until Monday morning. Alex and I wheeled the woman straight into the treatment room on a stretcher. Because she was in severe pain she took priority over all the other patients. The Duty MO was Capt 'Doc' Burgess, 3 Para's Doctor. He asked me to chaperone whilst he examined this lady, because Corporal Maggie Keating QARANC was busy dealing with a pregnant lady in Treatment Room 2. 'Doc' Burgess started asking relevant questions as he undid the lady's button and zip on her very tight jeans. He explained that she might have appendicitis and was going to check for rebound pain. Pressure is applied, using your fingers, above the groin to the side where the pain in coming from, you push down slowly and then release quickly, if the pain is increased sharply then the chances are you have appendicitis. As the 'Doc' applied some pressure the room was filled with the sound of a flock of seagulls taking off as the lady let rip with the loudest, wettest fart I have ever heard in my entire life. I started to laugh but soon stopped when my nostrils were filled with the stench of a mixture of over boiled sprouts, sweaty feet and silage. The fart was so loud that we could hear the patients in the waiting room laughing.

'Doc' Burgess looked up at me from the other side of the stretcher and said, "Corporal Clacy, would you be so good as to open that window behind you." The lady's face had taken on the colour of a Fire Engine but also the look of a woman who had just had her first orgasm. The relief she felt as the pressure was released was obvious. Unfortunately for her, she then had to walk out through the waiting room full of sniggering people.

On the Monday morning after the weekend's duty I was asked to prepare a Corporal from 22 Engineer Regt for his Pulheems examination because he was 30 years old. This mountain of a man was also flying out to Belize for a tour of duty the following day, so needed his medical to be rushed through rather than waiting until the afternoon when these types of medical examinations were usually done.

The family clinic was in full swing, with two wives and their small children being treated at the two medical examination couches in the main treatment room. Before doing his blood pressure, eye test and all the other pre examination tasks in the top treatment room, I took him into the main treatment room to get him a specimen glass so he could give me a sample of urine for testing. I apologised to Lynne, the Civilian State Enrolled Nurse, and asked if I could just get a specimen glass and enter his details in the treatment book.

"Yeah, it's ok Harry. None of the ladies in here are in a state of undress." I walked over to the sink next to where the specimen glasses and treatment book were located and handed the Corporal the glass with a paper towel covering it.

"Can you give me a sample of your urine in this, please. I'll enter your details in the treatment book." I then turned back to enter the relevant details into the book on the worktop whilst he went off to the toilets. After a couple of seconds I could hear the trickling sound of water, I looked behind me and saw the Corporal with his truncheon-sized knob out and pissing into the glass I had given him. The wives and children in the treatment room were stunned at the Corporal's brazen sample supply.

"What the hell are you doing?" I shouted. "I meant you to go to the gents toilet and give me a sample!"

His reply, in a concerned voice, was "Have you got another glass, mate, because this one is filling up." He then turned to his right, took his knob out of the glass and started pissing into the nurse's sink. He passed me the specimen glass, saying, "can you hold onto this for me?" After finishing his piss he shook his knob on the side of the sink, zipped him-self back up and put the paper in the flip top bin.

"What's next then?" he asked.

Ignorance of medical procedures was commonplace in all the patients who came to the Group Practice. I remember a Sergeant from my Squadron came down mid-morning one day with a sample bottle in a brown envelope. He asked for me in person and seemed rather sheepish as he whispered "I've got a sample for a sperm count that I've got to give in. Do I give it to you?"

"Yeah that's OK Sarge," I replied. "I'll put it in the fridge with the rest of the stuff going to the laboratory at RAF Wroughton."

He stayed close to me in the waiting room and whispered even lower.

"How much should there be in one go for a sample?"

I realised he was asking how much fluid should there be when a man ejaculates. I told him it depended on when you last ejaculated, whether your body had been exposed to cold temperatures, for instance when swimming, or the length of time you spent on the warm up period of sex before coming.

It was a strange question, so I said, "Why do you ask, Sarge?"

"Its taken me a week to fill that fucking thing up," he replied.

I started to laugh and put the sample in the bin and told him he would have to give a new sample, as there should only be one ejaculation in the sample bottle for testing.

"Fucking hell," he replied. "I can't do another one, my knob is red raw already and I've got a right forearm like bleedin' Popeye!"

Once you have completed a medical course of any kind, regardless of how trivial it is, neighbours automatically consider you to be an uglier version of Dr Kildare. They will assume you will have all the answers to any medical questions, even about brain surgery. I found that people started knocking on my door at all times of the day and night because they were unsure whether to bother the medical centre with their small problem. They obviously weren't concerned about bothering me!

One such neighbour lived next door but one, a six foot German blonde stick insect called Birgette. She had milk bottom glasses and green teeth and was the most hideous woman I have ever met in my life. She gave the word ugly a bad name. I was enjoying my tea of spaghetti Bolognese whilst watching the 6 o'clock news when she knocked on the front door yet again. Ronnie let her in and she asked, "Vould it pleeze being possible to be talking to Harry bitte?"

I put down my knife and fork, took a deep breath and asked, "What can I do for you this time Birgette?"

"I am having ze terrible piles in meine arsen and zey are much bleeding. Vould you possibly look at zem for me?"

Now, if she looked like Claudia Schiffer I would have had no hesitation in getting her to lie on the coffee table and have a good rummage around for her. But as she was more comparable with Claude Greengrass, I had difficulty in keeping my tea down. I told her to go and see her doctor in the morning.

In the Group Practice it was generally considered RMAs were not proper medics until they had delivered a baby in emergency childbirth. We had learned all the theory on the RMA Course and I felt when the time came I would be more than capable of dealing with the situation. I got my chance on a Sunday afternoon whilst on duty at the MRS when I was sent up to Perham Down Married Quarters to collect an RE Sapper's wife who was in labour. Her husband was away on exercise at the time so her friend, who seemed very relieved that I had arrived, met me at the door. The pregnant young lady told me she was due any day now and the pain in her lower back was getting very severe. This was her first pregnancy. The Duty MO told me to take her straight to RAF Wroughton hospital if I thought she was likely to go into labour within the next few hours. She was already in labour so I made the decision to head straight for the hospital. We walked her slowly to the ambulance and helped her into the back. Her waters broke as she started to lie back on the stretcher. Christ! It was like the Mohne dam after Wing Commander Guy Gibson had paid a visit. I told Alec, the ambulance driver, to get us to Wroughton as quickly as possible. I helped the young lady remove her underwear and got her into the most comfortable position. On the RMA Course we were told to give the impression of confidence to the patient at all times, regardless of how scared we were.

Trust me, I was shit scared.

It was approximately a 45-minute drive to RAF Wroughton hospital but with blue light flashing and horns blaring, I think Alec was trying to get there in 4 to 5 minutes. I did wonder why Alec was driving like a demented Greek taxi driver; it was her first baby and I felt sure she would be in labour for hours. It was at this point the patient said, "I think I want to start pushing, will that be alright?" I looked around the back of the ambulance to see whom she was talking to, but unfortunately I was the only one there. Shit! This was going to happen now and I was the unprepared idiot that was in charge. I examined her and noticed the crown of a head starting to come out as she started to push. I also noticed that I was sweating profusely. After the baby's head had come completely out I checked to make sure the umbilical cord was not wrapped around the neck and likely to caused complications.

Alec turned and shouted "We're almost there Harry!" through the driver's hatch. Those were the sweetest words I have ever heard in my life. He pulled up in front of the hospital, turned off the blue light and horns, the back doors flew open and I was faced with a very hostile female Flight Lieutenant nurse.

"Was that you making all that noise approaching the hospital?" she asked.

"No," I replied, "it was the horns on the top of the ambulance." As she started to give me a balling out an RAF doctor got in the back of the ambulance and completed the delivery. As the young lady was wheeled into the hospital with her newborn son she said to me, "Thank you so much, you were brilliant." Brilliant? The last 45 minutes of my life had gone past in a blur. I must have appeared a lot more confident than I really felt!

As I had only delivered a head, I was still not deemed to be a proper medic by some but I didn't care. I didn't, and still don't, fancy having to go through that again as long as I live.

Scary!

Bernie Wray arranged for all the RMAs to do a two week attachment at the A and E (Accident and Emergency) Department at Winchester Hospital. He thought dealing with real casualties would be a good experience for us. We had to do the attachment in pairs and I was matched up with a Lance Corporal called 'Geordie' from 2 RIR (Royal Irish Rangers), a really good RMA with a great sense of humour. We turned up at the hospital on the Monday morning at 0900 hours and introduced ourselves to the Charge Nurse, who was a John Inman lookalike but a lot more effeminate.

"Ooooh look girls, soldiers! All my birthdays have come at once!" he exclaimed.

'I am keeping well away from you old son,' I thought. 'There's no way you are going to unwrap *me*'. I really couldn't understand how someone so obviously camp would be given such a responsible job. He gave male nurses a bad name.

On the Friday of our first week there was a multiple pile-up on the bypass near Winchester. A fleet of ambulances attended and all the casualties came through our A and E. There were a few nasty head wounds and a lot of fractures, some of which were open. The hospital tannoy system requested extra doctors within the hospital who were not busy to come and assist in the A and E Department.

A doctor dashed into A and E in dramatic style and was completely out of breath. John Inman stood at the reception entrance and said, "OK Doctor, now calm down before you start scaring the patients. I want you to go into cubicle three and see to a teenage female casualty with a severe head injury. I will come and join you in a few moments to make sure everything is alright. OK, off you go. Nurse, I want you to go and get a bottle of Hartman's solution, a giving set and a 16-gauge canula and set it all up for the doctor in cubicle one, off you go now. Don't run! This is not an episode of Emergency Ward 10." He stood there and orchestrated the mayhem around him and never once raised his voice. He never panicked, he had answers to everything that was asked of him and reassured patients and staff alike. I was so impressed by this man and felt guilty about my first impression of him. If you were seriously injured, this would be the man you would want attending you.

"You two lovely boys can go into cubicle two and strip off the female with a head injury. Get her ready for the doctor to come and see," he told me and Geordie.

"I'm sorry," I said, "but Army policy states that RMAs cannot treat female patients whilst female staff are available."

He very firmly, but politely replied, "Well, now listen to me GI Joe, you are in the real world now. We don't have time for your silly little army protocol regulations, we are dealing with real people who are in real pain, so please go and prep the lady in cubicle two, we are very busy."

The lady in question was lying on the trolley in cubicle two and had a 3-inch gaping wound above her left eye. She was lucid, calm and spoke with a quite posh accent. I explained that were we going to have to undress her and put her in an operating gown so that the doctor could come and give her a thorough examination. She told me she was married to a doctor and had been trying to pick up a cassette tape on the floor of her car when the accident happened, she ran into the back of the vehicles that were involved in the main accident.

We put her clothes in a plastic bag to be stored under the trolley and I couldn't help but notice that she had a fantastic body. As I bent down to put her clothes under the trolley I noticed Geordie was staring at her and dribbling from the corner of his mouth.

"Geordie, we had better put a gauze dressing over that head injury ... Geordie? ... Geordie?" He seemed to snap out of his trance-like state, wipe his chin and start dressing the wound. The patient seemed a little embarrassed but made no comment as I helped her on with the gown. It seemed really strange having to deal with a naked female, particularly as she was so beautiful and try not to see her as a sexual person. I think if she had been decapitated Geordie probably wouldn't have noticed anything once her bra had been removed.

The following Monday we were asked if we wanted to attend a post mortem in the morgue at Winchester Hospital. We both jumped at the chance, mainly out of morbid curiosity, I suppose. The morgue was located near the A and E in what was on old hospital chapel, it was dark in there and one of the arch shaped windows was a multi coloured picture of some saint or other. There was a sickly smell in the cool building that the attendant explained was due to a body that had been bought in the previous weekend. An old gentleman had returned to his flat after doing some shopping, put on his gas fire, sat on his sofa and died. It was three weeks before the police broke down his front door after the neighbour reported not seeing him for a while. The mixture of the smells of rotting flesh and the chemical substances used in the morgue was overpowering.

A metal operating table at the far end of the morgue had a dead, naked 59-year-old gentleman on it. The mortician explained that he had been found dead in his office at work and no-one could account for what had happened to him; they were therefore having to carry out a post-mortem examination of the body. I hadn't actually seen a dead body before and felt a little nervous standing next to 'it'. I say 'it' because when you see a dead body there is no life; it really is an empty vessel. The body appeared waxy and had a blueish tinge. The chap who was carrying out the examination explained what he was going to do and said if we felt unwell at any stage we should go outside and get some fresh air. There was nothing to be ashamed of if we could not stomach a full post mortem. He made two incisions that formed a large X across the body and then proceeded to peel back the edges of skin to reveal the lower intestines and ribcage. I couldn't believe what I was seeing as he took a rotary saw to the ribcage so he could get a closer look at the heart and lungs. He seemed to enjoy the anatomy lecture he was giving us as he pointed out the heart and other vital organs of the human body.

I felt my throat start to constrict. I became increasingly nauseous, I started to sweat and became quite dizzy. This was the most surreal and disgusting event I had ever witnessed. I found it difficult to believe I was watching an, albeit dead, human being actually being carved up like a Christmas turkey. Geordie wanted to dive in up to his elbows as he found the whole process fascinating. I decided to take my leave and get some fresh air before I vomited into the cadaver's bowl-shaped cavity where his insides used to be. After 30 minutes of fresh air and 5 cigarettes I felt a lot better. Geordie told me later that the mortician believed the man had suffered a massive heart attack and more than likely died very quickly.

Six months after my attachment to Winchester Hospital, 66 Squadron was going to deploy on Exercise 'Amber Express' and as I had been medically upgraded to a PES (Pulheems Employment Standard) of P3 LE (Lines of Communication Everywhere) I was given permission to go on the Exercise with the Squadron. We were going to Denmark for the six-week NATO Exercise and I would be providing medical cover for the Squadron. It felt great to be more involved with the lads and going out in the field again, only this time I would be doing an entirely different job – a job I had grown to relish more than driving army trucks.

SSgt Derek Proudfoot RAMC was the Pharmacist at the Group Practice and with his help I put in my demands for the medical supplies I would require for the Exercise. The list was quite long and included:

Hartman's solutions (drips)
Giving sets and canulas
Antibiotics
Analgesics
Lignocaine 2% (Local Anaesthetic)
Sutures
Plaster of Paris Back Slab packs
Syringes
Surgical Spirit
Shell Dressings
Asilone Tablets
Laryngoscope
KY Jelly
Burns bags
Bandages
Micro-pore sticky tape
Sterile pre-packed instruments
Needles
Eyewashes

Dressings packs
Savlon solution
Rubber gloves
Scissors
Sphygmomanometer
Stethoscope
Scalpels
Steri swabs
Triangular Bandages
Pharyngeal Airways
Endotracheal tubes
Eye Washes
Kramer Splints

All these items were packed into a metal medical box that had a tray inlay for the smaller items. The Infantry RMAs gave me plenty of advice on packing items in the Medical Box and my own personal webbing as this was going to be my first exercise as a medic. This was also my first exercise as a diabetic, so I packed plenty of Mars bars and boiled sweets in my webbing and 58 Pattern large pack. I took two insulin injections a day, one before breakfast and the other before my evening meal, so my daily regime was quite simple. I had been given a light blue hard plastic box by BMH Rinteln that was designed to hold two vials of insulin, some needles and a plastic tube with a screw on top that held my glass insulin syringe in surgical spirit. This box fitted neatly into the left kidney pouch of my personal webbing. If I had to be detached from the Squadron for any length of time I could always take my insulin and stuff my face with Mars bars until I could get a proper meal. Doctors, Nurses and diabetic patients around the world will be holding their heads in horror at this, but it usually wasn't difficult to get a meal at different locations during the day.

My personal weapon within the Squadron was a 9mm SMG Sub Machine Gun (an updated version of the old Sten Gun). It was light and when the butt was folded away it wasn't too cumbersome. We drew weapons from the armoury at 'sparrows fart' (very early in the morning) and I was allocated an MK 4 tonner to travel in the back of with all the clerks from the Orderly Room. As soon as everyone was allocated their vehicles the Packets (Individual Convoys) departed Tidworth and headed for the port of Harwich to get on a DFDS (Danish Ferry Company) ferry that had been chartered by the MOD. As we pulled out of Jellalabad Barracks there was a mad scramble in the back of our wagon as everyone got out their dossbags, found a comfortable spot on some scrim nets and started knocking out the Z's.

On the ferry I was allocated a good cabin with Lance Corporal Jock Crowe, who was one of the Squadron clerks and a champion piss-taker. The food on the ferry was served in three restaurants; Officers and SNCOs had their own and the ORs (Other Ranks) ate in the main restaurant. The meals were buffet style and included lots of bread rolls, cheeses, cold meats and fruit. The crossing to Denmark was about 20 hours and we were allowed to drink alcohol from the bar but everyone was given the usual gypsy's warning about keeping it to a minimum, especially drivers of vehicles.

There is always one idiot who has to ruin it for everyone and our Squadron idiot got so pissed he fell down some stairs whilst returning to his cabin. A Troop Sergeant came to my cabin and told me to report to the SSM in the first aid room on the ship as he had a casualty for me. Outside the first aid room the SSM briefed me on what had happened and said the casualty had difficulty in breathing. If I thought he should be evacuated to a hospital by helicopter, it could be arranged. The SSM told me not to be swayed by what he thought but he felt the casualty was swinging the lead and if I agreed he was going to crucify the bastard. There was a very strong smell of booze in the room and the casualty was rolling about on the couch holding the left side of his ribcage and bleating how he could hardly breathe. I helped him remove his combat jacket and shirt and notice some abrasions to the left side of his chest. I got him to sit up straight and noted that there was no abnormality in the form of his ribcage. I listened to his lungs with my stethoscope and again noted no abnormality and I then carried out a physical examination. When I pushed on a certain area of his chest I asked if it was painful and he confirmed it was. I did this on several areas of his chest and returned back to the original spot and he stated there was no pain. He was obviously going through the usual Saturday night drunken theatrics. I turned to the SSM and said, "Where do you want the cross putting up Sir?"

The casualty spent the first week of the Exercise working in the Dixie Bash in the cook's tent.

We arrived at our unit location, not far from the city of Holbaek where we were co-located in a field with 22 Field Hospital, who had deployed from Aldershot. I was allocated a tent with five other blokes and I was pleased that one of them was Corporal Paul Paisey, because it was always a good laugh when he was around, although this was diluted with trepidation because Paul used to produce the foulest smelling farts of any British soldier; he really was quite proud of them. He told us that one night he had farted when in bed with his wife and had held her head under the duvet until she was gagging. She eventually threw up on the bedroom carpet. Poor old Sue left him for about three days after that, as she was so angry. Needless to say, everyone in the tent was rolling around with laughter at his story until he farted, when we all scrambled for the tent flaps and left him laughing on his own.

The SSM collared me about two weeks into the Exercise and ordered me over to the cooks tent where all units were being centrally fed and report to a cook sergeant who had cut his finger. The sergeant had a two-inch, very deep laceration that ran the length of his index finger. He had a couple of small plasters covering the wound but blood was constantly dripping from it. He had reported sick to 22 Field Hospital and they had just applied the plasters and fucked him off. I was surprised at his treatment and told him it needed suturing and I was prepared to do it for him if he wanted me to. He said, "Well I can't carry on like this so, yeah, if you can do it, let's get on with it."

I made sure he had a full range of movement in the finger without pain to make sure there was no ligament or tendon damage. I got a private to bring in some boiling water from the mobile kitchen and ordered him to scrub down one of the 6-foot trestle tables in the dining tent. I then sterilised the table with Surgical Spirit and laid out an NP 1 (a sterile Nursing Pack designed for changing dressings). After washing my hands and putting on some sterile rubber gloves I injected some 2% Lignocaine on the inside edges of the wound, then covered it with a gauze dressing and left it for about 10 minutes to go numb. Using a sterile needle I prodded around the wound and he confirmed that it was totally anesthetised. After washing the wound out with Hydrogen Peroxide I started suturing the wound.

I had done this on three different occasions in the Group Practice in Tidworth, under instruction from Bernie Wray. By this time I had attracted an audience and was enjoying the attention and answering questions ranging from, "How long will the anaesthetic last for?" to "Could you legally give a woman an emergency internal inspection?" The wound was neatly sealed with the sutures and no longer bleeding as I put on a firm dressing and wooden tongue depressor splint. I gave him some antibiotics and told him to keep it dry. I changed the dressings daily and took the sutures out about ten days later and he was left with a very small amount of scarring.

The cook sergeant asked me what I wanted for tea that night and when I said sirloin steak, egg and chips and a chocolate éclair for sweet he walked off laughing. That night while queuing up with everyone else for our evening meal, I was pulled out of the queue by the cook sergeant and told to go and sit in the dining area, as he was going to serve me my dinner. I don't know where he got the steak or chocolate éclair from, but they tasted wonderful.

All units had a day of R&R (Rest and Recuperation) in the city of Copenhagen about half way through the Exercise and we all jumped in the back of a 4-ton wagon for the hour and a half journey to the Danish capital. We were dropped off in a large car park at about mid-morning and told the last transport would be leaving at 2359 hours. If we were late and missed the transport 'tough shit', we would have to make our own way back to the Squadron location. We were really surprised to find, at 0200 hours the next morning, that there was no transport in the car park to take us back. The bastards really did mean it! Dvr Steve Pilling, a Yorkshireman from Mexborough, and I had spent the day and night touring as many bars and strip joints as we could find. He told me in his broad Yorkshire accent his two favourite Yorkshire jokes:

Joke number one:

Steve: "Ah bought a racing dog tuther dey".
Me: "Whippet?"
Steve: "No! ahv joost toled you, I fookin' bought it".

Joke number two:

Steve: "Ah bought a ginger cat tuther dey".
Me "Is it a tom?"
Steve: "No! ahv bought it wi me."

We had this music hall act down to a fine art and entertained anyone who would listen to us. We went through the same routine with a very attractive Danish barmaid, who seemed to get more confused as we went on. We had drunk a lot of beer by this stage though and were slurring and hiccupping our way through it.

Steve: "Ah bought a rayshing dog tuther dey.".
Me: "Washit a greyhound?"
Steve: "Nooo yer fookin prat, washit a fookin' whippet?"
Me: "Shorry mate, letsh do it again."
Steve: "Ah bought a rayshing dog tuther day."
Me: "Fakin' brilliant mate, wot's itsh name?"

Steve: "Noooo, for fooks sayke, I avn't really got a rayshing dog."

Me: "Well why the fak did you tell me you'd bought one then? You've never lied to me before shteve…"

When the barmaid wandered off to serve some other drunken soldiers further down the bar, Steve complained, "Fookin 'ell, I wash in there mate and you fooked it up for me you twat!"

Back in the car park I was with two lads from the Squadron and was in such a state I can't remember if one of them was Steve or not. Anyway, one of them went and stole an RMP motorbike that had been left unguarded on the street with the keys in the ignition. The guy who nicked the bike didn't know where the monkey was and cared even less. He drove all three of us back to the Squadron location on the bike and dumped it in a ditch full of water next to the Squadron camp. It was found the next day because the wheels could be seen poking out from under the water. The shit hit the fan, of course, but the monkeys couldn't prove who had done it, so the matter was dropped.

I was taken by the OC's Driver one day to a different location where one of our Drivers was complaining of a severe ear infection. The details were scant to say the least. Apparently Lance Corporal 'Scouse' Davies RCT, who was a trained RMA, was attending to him but asked if I could go and give some assistance. As we entered the Troop location I recognised 'Scouse', who had a Driver's head in his hands tilted to one side and was banging it against the wheel of a 4-tonner. The Driver had a black smudge down the right side of his face where his face had been scuffed against the tyre.

"What the fuck is going on Scouse?" I asked.

The driver's eyes seemed to be crossed and he looked like he had gone 10 rounds with Mike Tyson. He didn't have an ear infection, a small bug had crawled into his ear during the night and Scouse was trying to knock it back out again. I dissolved into fits of laughter and it took me about five minutes to regain control of myself and start treating the patient. I filled a 10ml syringe with some sterile water and flushed out the ear and was quite surprised by the size of the bug in his ear. It was still alive and kicking and must have been driving the patient insane as there was nothing he could do about the buzzing noise and tickling in his ear. The patient told me he still had a ringing in his ears but felt it was due to the treatment from Dr Scouse Davies, ENT (Ear Nose and Throat) Specialist.

When Endex (end of exercise) was called I was told I would be flying back to the UK with Paul Paisey and about six other

Drivers from the Squadron in an RAF VC10. We were flying into Brize Norton and would be picked up by a minibus from 66 Squadron. I noticed that a lot of soldiers in a particular RE unit were speaking in a Northern Irish accent and were boarding the same flight as us. I thought no more of it until we were coming in to land and the pilot announced over the aircraft intercom, “We are now approaching RAF Aldergrove Airport in Northern Ireland and will be landing in approximately 10 minutes.”

Paul Paisey shouted, “Fuck me! Not only have the RAF got the wrong Airport, they’ve got the wrong fucking country!”

The RE unit on the aircraft with us were all from the same TA unit in Northern Ireland and were being dropped off prior to our flight to Brize Norton.

The flight onward to Brize, in a massive VC 10 troop-carrying aircraft, had just eight passengers on board.

11. Chris

"The Paras are coming to Tidworth! The Paras are coming to Tidworth!" shouted Matthew as he came home from Castledown Secondary Modern School. All the children in Tidworth Garrison over the age of eleven went to Castledown School, near Ludgershall and the main topic of conversation was 3 Para. Matthew had always been army barmy since he had been given a toy gun, kiddie's combat uniform and a plastic soldier's helmet for his 5th birthday. In Tidworth, all the children had fathers who were soldiers; they saw them leave the house every day in various uniforms and forms of headdress. Yet all the kids were going nuts because Tidworth was now going to become home to 3rd Battalion of the Parachute Regiment. That is how much interest and enthusiasm the airborne forces can generate, even amongst Service Families.

I was firmly established in the Group Practice by the time 3 Para arrived in the Garrison and had become interested in Casualty Simulation work. This entailed putting make up and simulated wounds on soldiers so others could be tested on their First Aid skills. The makeup was great fun but we also had to brief our casualties on what their signs and symptoms were and how to react when treatment was given to them, either rightly or wrongly.

I was providing the casualty simulation expertise and helped run this side of an Infantry March and Shoot competition. Teams from Tidworth and Bulford Garrisons were tested at various stands on a timed competition route on Weapon, NBC, Medical, and Camouflage skills. My stand was the last part of the competition before the sections had to complete the shooting phase, we were therefore sited just to the rear of Tidworth/Bulford Ranges. All the simulated casualties I was making up were soldiers from the PWO (Prince of Wales Own Regiment of Yorkshire) who were the resident infantry battalion based in Bulford Garrison. Bulford is about six miles from

Tidworth. After each section had been tested and debriefed on their assessment, all the casualties had to be made up with fresh wounds, First Aid packs replenished and every one had to be ready for the next section to be tested. It was a very long, repetitive and tiring day.

The briefing to the Section Commander took the following format:

> *"There has been an off-road incident involving two unit Landrovers. There are a number of casualties who you must treat and prepare for evacuation as soon as possible. You may use all items in these two First Aid Packs and any equipment your section is carrying on you at the moment. All DS (Directing Staff) are wearing white armbands and carrying clipboards and are there to assess your treatment regimes, they cannot give you any help or advice. There are no tactical implications or threat from any enemy forces. If a member of the Directing Staff shouts "STOP"! Everyone in the section must stop what they are doing and await further instructions (This was made clear in case our casualties were being put in any danger). Do you have any questions? You now have two minutes to brief your section before the exercise begins."*

The casualties were a mixture of head, abdominal injuries and open and closed fractures. We usually put an unconscious casualty just out of sight to see if the Section Commander did a sweep of the area to make sure they hadn't missed anyone. The driver of one of the Landrovers could prompt the Section Commander by asking what happened to his mate because he hadn't seen him since the accident. Each DS noted the Section number on his marking sheet and the final marks were sent over to the competition HQ to be registered on their scoreboard.

It was about an hour to lunchtime and we had two sections to test before we got an hour's break before starting the afternoon session. Sitting on a rock, to the side of the incident area, was a paratrooper watching what we were doing. When he stood up, I noticed he was about 5 foot 10, had an athletic physique with a jaw and chin like Desperate Dan. He was good looking, with a typical military moustache of the 1980s. He seemed to lope over to me rather than walk, held out his hand, gave a very firm handshake and said, "I'm Chris Lovett, 3 Para. You're pretty good at this aren't you?" I was flattered that someone thought I was good at anything; soldiers normally slag you off, even if they are impressed with what you are doing.

I showed him how we made up an open fracture wound on a casualty's arm and he seemed to be really interested and asked if he could have a go. Chris told me he was a member of 3 Para's Medical Team and would be working in the Group Practice in Tidworth. He said he fancied learning more about casualty simulation. Chris told me he had been allocated a Married Quarter just up the road from where mine was and said he would bring his wife Michelle round one night for a few beers and we could talk about Casualty Simulation. Chris was stood behind one of the casualties I was making up and the guy said that the PWO had been selected for a NATO skiing exercise in Norway because his battalion were better prepared than 3 Para for the job.

"Yeah! Course they are mate," Chris said. "Your mob have to use skis cos they're too fucking fat to run. You Knob!"

The PWO started mumbling under his breath and Chris poked his tongue in and out of his cheek and used his hand to simulate an oral sex act. That said it all as far as Chris was concerned. He winked at me and said he would see me later and ran off towards the car park. It occurred to me later that he had probably noted all the casualties and set off to inform 3 Para's Sections what they were about to face. I was in awe of Chris as he oozed self-confidence and although he had a casual manner you knew not to fuck him about. He had such a friendly attitude towards me that I almost felt honoured that he hadn't called me a Crap Hat. In fact, Chris never called me a Crap Hat in all the time I knew him. I could never understand why he selected me as a friend.

As far as I can remember the top two sections were from 2 RIR and 3 Para but I can't remember, in all honesty, which unit actually won the competition.

When I got home for tea I told to Ronnie about this Paratrooper called Chris who I had met and explained that he would like to call round one evening with his wife and have a drink. She seemed OK about it and said that if I saw him at work we should arrange something for next week. We had just cleared the dishes from tea into the kitchen when there was a knock on the door. It was Chris and his wife Michelle. If Chris planned to do something he would always do it straight away; no point in waiting till next week.

Michelle was a young, slim and very attractive woman with shoulder-length, straight, blonde hair. I have never met a paratrooper with an ugly woman unless they were on a 'Grab a Grot' night (this involved every soldier taking part trying to get off with the fattest and ugliest female in the bar. Votes from those participating were counted to decide the winner). Michelle was very quietly spoken, always avoided eye contact and appeared to be very shy. She was polite and intelligent but very reserved and seemed to apologise for anything and everything.

They brought their two sons Peter and Ben round with them and both had their mother's blonde hair, cut in a short military manner. Peter and Ben looked like a couple of angels whose mouths wouldn't melt butter, but I would find out later that they were a mischievous couple of little sods, just like their dad! Peter was the same age as our son Daniel, in fact they shared the same birthday. Chris told me he had delivered both his boys at home in his Married Quarter. When Peter, the oldest boy, was born in Osnabruck, Germany, Chris refused to let the medical team into the flat until he had completed the delivery. Thinking back to how I had felt delivering that head of a baby in the ambulance on the way to Wroughton, I realised how much bottle and confidence Chris had in everything he did. If Chris had been in the back of that ambulance he would probably have told the Flight Lieutenant Nurse to pop off and make him a cup of tea as he was a bit too busy to deal with her.

Chris was a terrific medic. He seemed to absorb medical information like a sponge and wanted to learn anything that would be of use in field medicine. He always remained calm and in control during any medical emergency. We helped out at an RTA (Road Traffic Accident) at the crossroads at the bottom of Station Road in Tidworth one day. By the time the police and ambulance service had arrived Chris had detailed two soldiers from 2 RGJ to control the traffic. Chris and I dealt with a middle-aged woman who was travelling in one car on her own. She had got out of her car in a distressed state and collapsed about 10 meters from the accident. She had a small cut on her forehead and was so upset that she was sobbing about attending her son's sports day. Chris grabbed a first aid kit full of army shell dressings from his car and told me to put a dressing on the lady's forehead. He made sure the lady didn't have any other injuries or loss of feeling in any extremities, checked her pupils to make sure they were even and confirmed she didn't have a head injury. He spoke to the casualty in a calm and casual manner and acted as if he had known the woman for years. He told her everything was going to be OK and not to worry because she was in the hands of the 3rd Battalion of the British Army's airborne infantry and in safe hands now.

She seemed to calm down quite quickly but as we helped load her into the civilian ambulance the shell dressing I had put on her forehead came loose and fell on the stretcher pillow. Chris looked at me and said "Knob! Why didn't you use a crepe bandage to keep it in place?" I felt totally chastised, and quite rightly too, as I had failed to complete the most basic of first aid tasks correctly. In later years I would often used this story when teaching lessons on the treatment of bleeding wounds. I would shout at students and tell them what a 'knob' they were because they "couldn't even put on a fucking shell dressing properly." It was a good teaching aid.

As time went by, Chris and I became very good friends and on a few occasions at 1000 hours, after morning Sick Parade, we would go to his house, play chess and enjoy a brew and half a dozen cigarettes. I only ever won about a handful of games of chess against him, as he was an astute tactician. Being a conscientious soldier at the time, I would say to Chris "What if someone was looking for us at the Group Practice mate, we could be in deep shit for skiving."

His answer was simple. "Fuck 'em!"

He really meant it as well.

I always tried to remain fit, even though the Medical Board advised me not to do the BFT (Basic Fitness Test), which was a running test all soldiers had to complete twice yearly. We had to run a mile and a half in a squad in 15 minutes exactly and then a further mile and a half as an individual in under 11 minutes. This was done wearing boots, denims and a PT vest. Right up to my last BFT before leaving the army I had never failed a BFT or wimped out of attending one.

Chris asked me if I wanted to go running with him one day and I said, "You have to be joking mate. I could never keep up with you." I told him of my embarrassing failure on the 'beat up' but he told me not to worry because his knees were shot to shit after some bad parachute landings. I was also worried about having hypoglycaemic attacks if we went too far.

"Leave it to me, I'll sort something out," he said.

We left the Group Practice at 1600 hours in PT kit and Chris was wearing a 58-pattern belt with two water bottles full of very sweet orange juice in them and an ammo pouch stuffed with Mars bars. We ran on a triangular route on the A3026 into Ludgershall, turned left onto the A342 for the same distance and then left again onto the A338 back into Tidworth. A total distance of 7 miles, which for a paratrooper is just a walk in the park, but for a 24-year-old RCT truckie, who had started to develop a bit of a diabetic paunch, it was going to be difficult, to say the least.

The first part of the run was up a bastard of a hill that seemed to be like climbing the North face of the Eiger. On our first run I got to about half way up the hill before I had to stop. Chris encouraged me to carry on, as we hadn't gone very far. He said I should ignore the pain and think of something else to take my mind off it. He kept my blood sugar up by constantly feeding me Mars bars and drinks of orange juice.

That first run was a nightmare and I didn't fancy doing any more, but the following day I was to meet Chris at the Group Practice again at 1600 hours for another 7-mile run. At one minute past 1600 hours Chris hadn't turned up, so I drove home, thinking he would go for a run on his own and I could slag him off the next morning for not turning up at the designated time. I drove home and was in the process of telling Ronnie my plan when I saw Chris running up the path towards my house like the Terminator pursuing his human prey. I told Ronnie to answer the door and tell him she didn't know where I was because I was too knackered to go for another run. When she answered the door and Chris asked where I was, Ronnie replied, "He's hiding in the kitchen."

After two months of running every day with Chris I had slimmed down two trouser sizes and my fitness was as good as anyone in my Squadron and probably a lot better than the majority of them. Unfortunately, 3 Para went on a tour of Belize and I didn't have the self-discipline to continue with the running and the weight came back on in no time at all.

In Tidworth the Brigade Commander had a serious problem with 3 Para and 2RIR serving in the same Garrison; they spent so much time beating each other up that he decided each would serve a consecutive 6-month tour in Belize. That way the Garrison would have at least one complete year of relative peace. The plan worked well until 3 Para flew out to relieve 2 RIR. One company from each unit met at a civilian airport in America whilst the planes were refuelled and they had a couple of hours stopover. A Ranger shouted to a Para, "We're going back to Tidworth to fuck all your wives!" The Para calmly shouted back, "That seems only fair, because for the last six months we've been trying to fuck some sense into all of yours!" The inevitable fight erupted, much to the consternation of all the civilians in the airport.

The 3 Para Medical Team was made up of Capt John Burgess RAMC who was the MO, Sgt Steve Bradley took over from CSgt Brian Faulkner as the RMA Team Leader. The rest of the team consisted of Corporals John Sibley, Phil Proberts and Keith Cope, Lance Corporal John Kennedy, Chris, Pte Mark Dodsworth and a bloke I can only remember being called Ash. They were the most robust RMA team in Tidworth.

As I was driving away from the Group Practice in my car to go for lunch one day, I shouted to John Kennedy, "Oi! You with the pink hat on!" John was a martial arts student, he chased and kept up with me whilst I was changing from 2nd to 3rd gear and was trying to punch me through the open side window of my car whilst shouting "Come back you Crap Hat coward!" How I got away with the liberties I took I shall never know.

I was Duty Driver for the Group Practice one day, which involved driving the black army Mini on any details around the Garrison area. Cpl Phil Proberts asked me if I could give some of the lads a lift down to the Rose and Crown pub in Everleigh at about 1100 hours.

"Sure mate, not a problem," I said. "I'll meet you outside in a couple of minutes."

I went and collected the mail from Bernie Wray's office and headed outside to the Mini. I couldn't believe my eyes. There were four paratroopers crammed in the back of the car and Phil was in the passenger seat shouting, "Come on Harry, we're fucking gagging for a pint!"

I couldn't see the top of the Mini's tyres as there was so much weight pushing the body of the vehicle down. The car was on the point of stalling every time I tried to pull away in 1st gear so I had to use the revs and clutch quite aggressively until I built up enough speed to maintain a forward motion.

As I dropped them off at the pub, John Kennedy said, "Pick us up at 1400 hours and don't be late!" Necky bastard.

I arrived to pick them up at about 1400 hours and they were nowhere to be seen. On entering the pub I saw them all propping up the bar and having a good laugh, John Sibley said, "Ah! Here is our Crap Hat Driver. Take us home would you my good man." They were all pissed as farts and took the Mickey all the way back to Tidworth.

John Sibley and Chris had been very good friends for years and were drinking buddies. John asked Chris if he would be a nominated driver on his insurance so he could do some of the driving when they went on the razz together in his white Jaguar XJ6. He agreed but John had to pay the premium. It was high because of the type of car and as John was on a higher rate of pay as a full screw and was a single soldier he could afford it. Chris was a Lance Jack with a wife and young family to support. John gave Chris the cash to put himself on the insurance. The insurance office was next to the Lloyds

Bank up the top of Station Road. At the bottom of the road was a General Store where you could buy anything from a pair of Wellington boots to a fridge. As Chris walked up towards the insurance office he looked in the General Store window and noticed a second hand colour TV set and thought 'Michelle and the boys would love that'. They didn't have a television at home and it was exactly the same price as the cost of the nominated driver insurance. He thought 'I'm a good driver, the chances of me having an accident are reasonably low, Michelle and the kids would love a TV, fuck it… He went in and bought the TV and told John they didn't give him a cover note and that it was more than likely in the post.

Unfortunately, within a couple of days Chris had wrapped the Jaguar XJ6 round a lamp post and got a nasty cut near his left eye in the process. The Police and Ambulance Services were in attendance. When asked for insurance details Chris told the Police Officer he didn't have any but he did have a colour TV set. John Sibley was furious, as his car had to be written off, but as he and Chris were such good friends the whole thing blew over very quickly.

The first time I went out on the lash with Chris he turned up at my house in his orange VW Variant and told Ronnie we were going to meet the rest of the 3 Para Medical Team up at The Drummer Pub.

"Make sure you bring him back alive," she told him.

As we got in Chris's car he leaned into the back, grabbed a pair of army pyjamas and threw them on my lap.

"You'll need these for tonight," he said. "We ain't going to the Drummer mate, we're going to a pyjama party at the nurses digs next to the MRS."

I had no idea he had planned this and felt a little uneasy at the thought of being dishonest to Ronnie when we returned. But what the hell … if I was going to be in the shit, I might as well enjoy it. The house where the nurses all lived was packed with loads of gorgeous women in various stages of undress or wearing very skimpy and silky nightwear. It was a voyeur's dream come true. I could not believe these women were squeezing past me wearing next to nothing in the crowded passageways and corridors. We had a very drunken night out with lots of lechery and leering, but that was as far as it went. None of these women were going to be interested in me when there was a house full of Paras to choose from. Chris drove us home at about 0200 hours after an absolutely brilliant night.

I have been told by a lot of Royal Marine Commandos that they believe themselves to be a thinking man's Paratrooper. Some of them believe the Paras to be just mindless thugs. Contrary to a lot of Marines' views, I found Paras to be quick witted and articulate, but very aggressive. You were never sure when talking to one of them if they were taking the piss out of you.

Chris was having a pint in the Rose and Crown at Everleigh on a Sunday afternoon, wearing the off duty Para uniform of maroon sweatshirt with 3 Para logo on it, jeans and desert boots. In the pub were four lads from 2 RIR and they started taking the piss out of Chris. He went over to them, introduced himself and asked what unit they were from. He offered to buy them a pint and asked if they fancied going on the piss with him for the afternoon. Three declined, as they were off back to camp, but the fourth lad was persuaded to stop for another pint and Chris said he would drop him back in Tidworth afterwards. Chris talked to him about parachuting and the lad seemed to be enthralled at what Chris had to say.

After finishing their pints, Chris said, "I'm just off for a quick piss. I'll meet you outside at my car, it's the orange VW Variant in the car park." Chris had his piss and went out to the car park, where he saw the lad leaning on his car. He went straight up to him and snarled in his face "What the fuck are you doing leaning on my car?" Chris told me he could see the penny drop in the look on the lad's face. He had been suckered into a trap and his other three mates were not there to help him. Chris filled him in and relished it as he told him never to take the piss out anyone from 3 Para again. He got in his car but then thought it would be a good idea to finish off his performance by actually driving over the top of his victim. Fortunately for Chris, the lad scrambled out of the way, because he could have killed him instead of just breaking his ankle. Chris came to my house immediately after doing this and as I let him in he said, "If anyone asks, I've been here all afternoon, OK mate?"

If there had been even the slightest chance of getting Chris out of this I would have lied under oath to help him out, but there were witnesses to the ambush. The civilian police approached Chris about the incident and said it would have to go to Crown Court, as the injured lad was not an Irish Ranger, he was a civilian.

As it went through the slow process of the British Judicial system, the Argentine Army invaded the Falkland Islands and 3 Para were one of the units mobilised to restore them to British rule. I was still working in the Group Practice and went to 3 Para's Medical Stores with Chris one evening to watch them prepare all their medical stores for the war. Chris told me before the invasion had happened that he was fed up with the Airborne Forces and wanted to do a less military operational job and had applied to join the RAMC as an OTT (Operating Theatre Technician). He was granted the transfer and was waiting for a course date before he would be transferred to the RAMC. The Invasion of the Falkland Islands changed all that. Chris firmly believed there was going to be a war and he wanted to be in on it. He was told the transfer would be delayed until he returned from the South Atlantic and his outstanding court case would have to wait as well.

Chris came to my house after saying goodbye to Michelle and the boys and I gave him a lift down to Candahar Barracks with his webbing, Bergen and 9mm SMG. I dropped him at the guardroom and helped him get his very heavy kit out of the back of my Datsun Estate car. He shook my hand and said, "See you when I get back mate."

I don't believe in premonitions of any kind. I also don't believe in the spirit world or the charlatans who make money out of other people's sadness, but as I stood there watching Chris walk away towards whatever fate held in store for him, I had a strong feeling that I would never see him again.

I had attended a couple of Medical Boards in the preceding months and was told I would have to leave the RCT, as I could no longer fulfil my role as an HGV driver. The RMA job was only a sideline within the RCT and I had to move on.

I had got to know a lot of the staff in the Dental Centre and they told me the RADC (Royal Army Dental Corps) were always looking to recruit people from other Corps to fill their ranks. I went for an interview and was granted a transfer and given a date to attend a Course at the RADC Depot on the Queens Avenue in Aldershot.

My mate Johnny Walker had been posted from 10 Regt to JSHSU (Joint Services Helicopter Support Unit) and was based at RAF Odiham, not far from Aldershot. His unit were known as the 'Happy Hookers' as their job was to organise and hook up netted cargo loads on the undersides of helicopters. I hadn't seen him for a while and was surprised to see him one afternoon sitting on my bed in the Dental Corps accommodation block. I was always pleased to see my best mate, as he was great fun to be with, but today he seemed more reserved than his usually over-the-top manner.

"I thought you might like to get out of this dump for a while and get some beer down our necks," he said.

It sounded a great idea to me and we went back to his ground floor flat in Wilhelm's Park in Aldershot. We knocked back a couple of tins of beer as he talked about his new unit and took the piss out of me for being a Dental Corps wanker. All of a sudden his mood changed and he said, "I got a phone call from Ronnie, mate, and I've got some bad news for you. She said she couldn't face telling you herself and asked me to do it. Your mate Chris Lovett was killed in the Falklands two days ago. I am so sorry."

I was stunned. I felt sick in my stomach and started to sob uncontrollably. Not Chris. He was indestructible. Johnny sat on the sofa with me and put his arm round my shoulder and tried to say all the right things to placate me, but my grief was overwhelming. Johnny telephoned Ronnie back in Tidworth so I could speak to her and confirm what had happened. She apologised for being such a coward about not telling me the bad news and told me that Pte Mark Dodsworth, who was also on the 3 Para Medical Team, had also been killed. Mark had only been married a short while before going down to the Falklands. I asked after Michelle and the boys and Ronnie assured me she was being given all the help she needed by friends and the Rear Party.

Chris and I had not known each other very long in comparison to a lot of his friends in 3 Para but I felt so close to him. He was the sort of man I wanted to emulate; the sort of man I wanted as a brother. Now he was gone and there was nothing I could do about it. I wish I had stopped him as I dropped him at Candahar Barracks when he left for the Falklands and told him how much I looked up to him and how much he meant to me. But now it was too late.

I don't want to paint Chris as a paragon of virtue, because he wasn't. He was an intelligent but tough guy who anyone with an ounce of common sense would not mess with. Twenty-seven years after Chris was killed I still think about him and make people laugh at some of the outrageous stunts he got involved in. He had his faults, and plenty of them, but he made me his friend and for that I feel deeply honoured.

After the war was over, the Next of Kin were given the option of having their deceased husbands and sons returned to the UK for burial and Michelle chose to have Chris bought home to Worthing, where he was born and raised as a young man. Michelle asked me if Ronnie and I would like to attend Chris's funeral, along with Corporal Dave Turner, an RAMC Medic who had also served in the Falklands War. Dave and Chris were also good friends and drinking buddies.

I had transferred to the RADC by the time of the funeral and had to attend in Number 2 Service Dress, wearing the RADC 'Twat Hat' (similar to a Reg Varney bus driver's hat) that had a green band around it. Apart from Chris's brother, who was serving in the RAF at the time, I think Dave Turner and I were the only Crap Hats at the funeral.

After Chris was lowered into the ground and the last post had been played, Dave and I waited our turn and marched up to the grave, halted and saluted in unison. I could hear Ronnie behind me say, "Oh my god" and she started to cry.

In the local town hall, a wake was held after the funeral and Dave and I chatted to all the Paras who had come down to Worthing for the funeral and a lot of banter was flying back and forth. One of them had obviously had a word with young

Peter and Ben because the little sods were dancing round the hall singing *"Harry is a Crap Hat! Harry is a Crap Hat!"* – much to the amusement of the 3 Para Medical Team.

I know Chris would have laughed as well.

This was the official citation for Chris's award for gallantry during the Falklands War:

> ***24355078 Lance Corporal Christopher Keith Lovett***
> ***Mention in Despatches***
>
> *Lance Corporal Lovett was the medical assistance with A Company throughout operations ashore. In this capacity, he greatly contributed to the maintenance of the fighting efficiency and morale of the Company. Thus the casualty rate from feet and other ailments was kept extremely low, despite arduous weather conditions and distances covered on foot.*
>
> *On the night of 11/12 June 1982, the Company was ordered to capture the Northern Ridge of Mount Longdon. Once the Company were under fire, and began to take casualties, Lance Corporal Lovett would selflessly expose himself to enemy fire in order to reach and tend casualties. Later the same night, he moved with the Company onto the summit of the mountain. The task of the Company was to capture the Eastern pinnacle of the feature, and Lovett continued to act with great bravery as the platoons advanced from objective to objective. It was whilst once again running to the assistance of a casualty, over an open saddle of ground swept by enemy direct fire, that he was killed by a sniper. His bravery, professional dedication and selfless conduct throughout this major battle reflected his outstanding performance throughout the campaign. His behaviour was in the highest traditions, and merits special recognition.*

When the lads from 3 Para Medical Team returned from the South Atlantic, I called in to the Group Practice to see them; they told me that Chris had been killed when an Argentine shell exploded next to the 3 Para Regimental Aid Post near the base of Mount Longdon. He was the only one standing as the shell exploded because he was moving from casualty to casualty, checking their dressings and drips and trying to make them as comfortable as possible. None of the prone casualties near him suffered any other injuries from that shell. A cease-fire was agreed two days later.

12. Revenge

When I moved into my Married Quarter in Tidworth I noticed my next-door neighbour was a broad-shouldered, tall woman with short blonde hair. She looked like an Australian female surfer. The family was made up of herself, a daughter, aged six, who was a carbon copy of her mother and a demented four-year-old boy whose total vocabulary consisted of repeating "I need the toilet, toilet, toilet, TOILET!" The mother was polite but seemed a bit downtrodden. At lunchtime I found out why; she was married to Sergeant Brewer of 2 RGJ, the miserable bullying bastard who had made me stand in a ditch of frozen water for 40 minutes in South Armagh. I recognised him straight away and when his wife tried to introduce us over the garden fence he just grunted and said "Wot are we 'avin for lunch, I'm starving." There was not a flicker of recognition on his face when he looked at me, he had obviously been such a twat to so many people that I was probably just one of many soldiers who hated his guts. Ronnie was quite a keen amateur gardener at the time and discussed a range of horticultural subjects with Sgt Miserable Bastard's wife. She told Ronnie the reason she grew so many carrots was that they were her husband's favourite vegetable. (I would have thought his favourite vegetable would have been his son, but you live and learn.) The rows and rows of carrots were planted up against the wire-dividing fence between our gardens and Ronnie told me of everything the Australian surfer had rather unknowingly let slip about her husband's penchant for carrots. I had an idea.

When 2 RGJ were posted over to West Germany from Tidworth I was sorry to say goodbye to Corporal Bob Buckland and the lads but glad to be getting rid of the prat next door. They had packed up their Married Quarter and had cleaned it up ready for handover, their new tax-free car was parked right outside the house with the boot open and suitcases packed inside. They were busy inside going through the last bits and pieces of the handover so I decided to pop a white envelope addressed to SGT BREWER 2 RGJ under the bottom suitcase, no doubt he found it while unpacking his car when he arrived in his new Garrison. The letter read:

My dearest Sgt Brewer,

I have lived next door to you for the last eighteen months and you have never had the decency to pass the time of day with me or any of your neighbours. You probably don't even know you served with me in Northern Ireland, where you proved what a cruel and miserable James Hunt you were to me personally and probably many other soldiers as well.

Your wife told us you like your carrots and have them with most of your meals. Did you know that as a root vegetable it absorbs a lot of moisture from the ground to make it grow? Well I thought I would give your wife a helping hand every night as I had my last cigarette in the garden before going to bed. For the last eighteen months I have been pissing on your vegetables every night. I often wonder if it gave them a tangy taste, perhaps you could write and let me know.

This is probably the most childish thing I have done in my entire life but it amused me no end. Please feel free to take this letter to the Royal Military Police and see if they can stop laughing long enough to use it as evidence to charge me under Section 69 of the Army Act 1955 with, 'Conduct unbecoming of a Junior Non Commissioned Officer".

Please give my commiserations to your new neighbours and try to be nice to them and they might not do something nasty to get back at you.

I remain, Sergeant
Your Disobedient Slasher
Harry Clacy RCT
Lance Corporal

The Royal Military Police in BAOR never got in contact so I presume he thought better of approaching them.

13. Everyone has a War to Fight

I was now on my course in Aldershot to become a DCA (Dental Clerical Assistant), which involved being a Dental Nurse as well as a clerk running the administration in the Dental Centre office. The Course was made up of only four people; apart from me it consisted of the following:

Corporal Jeff Bush, who was transferring from the DERRs (Duke of Edinburgh's Royal Regiment (Infantry) was a fellow West Ham United supporter and would go on to become the RADC WO 1 RSM. Jeff told me that he hated all RCT soldiers because when he was a young Private on Exercise in West Germany, he had once been on guard in a trench filled with cold water and it was pouring with rain. On the other side of the track he noticed a parked RCT 4-Tonner; its engine was running with the cab heater on the hottest setting and all the windows were steamed up. The two Drivers inside were enjoying large mugs of steaming hot sweet tea when Jeff crossed over the track and knocked on the cab door. The window was opened to a gap of about three inches and he could just see a pair of lips with a large bushy moustache above them. The Driver, angry at being disturbed said "Wot?" Jeff was shivering in the cold and said "Alright mate! My name is Jeff Bush, I'm a Private with the Duke of Edinburgh's Royal Regiment. I'm on stag in that trench over there and I'm fucking freezing. Could you give me just a sip of your brew?" The large bushy moustache had hesitated and then replied... "Nah! Fuck off!"

Private 'Pip' Green had served as a clerk in the Royal Artillery before transferring to the RADC. He was then discharged from the army after serving 3 years and became a milkman. He found life in Civvy Street boring and unrewarding, so decided to re-enlist into the RADC and give it another try. 'Pip' could play the guitar quite badly. He wrote and sang his own dirges, two of which I remember; one was about the Pennlee lifeboat disaster and the other about an old whore called

Annie who no-one wanted to shag anymore. When he was posted to Hildesheim he offered his talents at the Garrison theatre night. Anyone who could do a skit or entertain in any way was encouraged to perform on stage, in front of the rest of the Garrison. 'Pip' did a spot in the first half of the evening and sang the above two songs. He was applauded and walked off stage to have a beer. Later on in the second half of the evening the compere came back on stage after an act had just finished and said "Thank you Sergeant Sheilds. I've never seen anyone juggle their balls with such dexterity. Would you all now put your hands together and welcome back on stage Private 'Pip' Green, who will sing us some more of his own compositions" at which point a drunken soldier at the back of the hall shouted "Oh no! Not that morbid bastard again!"

Lance Corporal Paul Harratt was an RAMC medic who was pissed off with his own Corps and decided to try the RADC to see if his promotion chances would be any better. Paul was a Yorkshireman who looked like a Mexican bandit. He had an athletic and muscular physique and was a good lad who would help anyone out of a fix. I loss contact with Paul after we completed our initial DCA Course but kept in touch with Jeff and 'Pip' until I came out of the army.

We all got on like a house on fire and I can't remember when I laughed so much in my army career. We took the piss out of the wankers within the RADC and each other.

Our introduction to the Corps was in the form of Sergeant Rolfe, who was to be our main instructor throughout the entire Course. He was an ex Light Infantryman who had transferred into the RADC and was an excellent instructor. He was a very smart and fit-looking SNCO. The four of us sat in a classroom on the first day of the Course and he came in, introduced himself to us and said, "Everyone's got a war to fight and from now on yours will be against tooth decay."

We burst out laughing. He was under no illusions about the military role of the RADC, don't get me wrong, but anyone who has had toothache will understand the necessity of a dentist when you are in pain. In fact, the Dental Corps was formed not long after the First World War because during the war Field Marshall Haig had toothache and had to see a

French dentist because the British Army didn't have one in its ranks. In the pecking order of the army though we lay firmly at the bottom because most other cap badges viewed us as a bunch of fairies, but in fact the RADC was made up of about 50% of TFIs (Transfers In) from just about every Corps and Regiment in the British Army. The whole Corps numbered about 600 strong, which is about the size of an average Infantry Battalion.

The course involved learning the anatomy of the human skull and all the teeth and muscles of mastication. When I commented, "As far as I know, there is only one muscle of masturbation," it was pointed out they were talking about masti*cation* which is chewing. They were not talking about pulling your pud. We also had to learn how to record a dental inspection on the relevant charts, take dental x-rays, type, use some of the dental equipment in the surgeries and how to make dental models from impressions.

Some of the lessons given by the Lieutenant-Colonel dentists were so boring it was difficult to stay awake. I nodded off one day and the Lt-Col asked "Am I boring you Lance Corporal Clacy?"

"No sir!" I lied. "I'm really sorry but I am diabetic and I think I'm having a hypoglycaemic attack."

He went into serious panic mode and told Jeff to take me down to the coffee and chocolate machines and get me something to eat. After we had left the classroom Jeff asked me if I was OK. I told him I had just fallen asleep and thought the low blood sugar excuse was a good idea. We left Paul and 'Pip' to enjoy the rest of the lesson on Chronic Inflammatory Periodontal Disease whilst we had a 20-minute break.

We also had to learn how to give oral hygiene lessons to soldiers individually and in groups; this was done using a model of a set of teeth that was about the size of a dinner plate and a 12-inch toothbrush. All this had to be done and tests passed before we were allowed onto the Clinical Wing and work in the surgeries alongside the dentists who treated all the troops in the Aldershot Garrison.

On Jeff's first day on the Clinical Wing he was working with a Lt-Col who had just given a dental inspection to a very tough-looking sergeant from Depot Para.

"Corporal Bush, take this sergeant to the DHE (Dental Health Education) room and teach him how to clean his teeth properly will you."

Jeff grabbed his oversized set of teeth and toothbrush and showed the sergeant the way to the DHE room. Once outside the surgery the sergeant growled, "Is he taking the fucking piss?" Jeff felt really stupid having to teach a tough, trained killer how to clean his teeth properly, so he said to the Para "Shall we go for a fag instead Sarge?" They both sat on the Fire Exit steps for the next ten minutes whilst the Para smoked a cigarette and Jeff told him about his days in the infantry, just to prove he wasn't a mincing great fairy.

The Course proved to be the least taxing and most boring thing I had done since joining the Army. I hated it in this new role and found a lot of the SNCOs who had not served outside of the RADC to be stuck up their own arseholes. One particular WO2 in the depot strutted around and bitched at people of a lower rank like an old washerwoman; he pissed me off so much that I sneaked, undetected, into the depot after work and gained access to his office. I made a gentian violet and glycerol paste (gentian violet is an antifungal powder that stains everything purple) and smeared it around the earpiece of his telephone. When he came into work the following morning I was working on the reception desk. I saw him go into his office and I rang his telephone extension. I know it was childish, I know as a JNCO I should have behaved in a more adult and serious manner, but to see him walking around for a week with a purple ear made him look an even bigger twat than he really was.

The whole incident was blown up into something resembling the Nuremberg War Trials but as I had got in and out of the depot unseen no one knew who had done the dirty deed. I felt sorry for the Duty NCO who was on duty that night as he copped an earful (pardon the pun) from the RSM. Every time I bumped into the 'twat' I had to bite my lip to stop myself from laughing. He was a very angry purple-eared fairy.

On completion of the DCA 3 Course the three of us had to go to the Garrison Clothing Store to exchange our cap badges, lanyards and staple belts. The guy running the store was a good bloke and he said we could keep at least one of our old Corps and Regimental cap badges as a memento.

It was a warm and sunny day when Jeff and I came out of the store wearing our new RADC cap badges. Jeff looked at me, shivered, started to rub his arms and said, "Fucking hell, it's freezing today isn't it?" We were now established Tooth Fairies.

I was posted back to Tidworth after finishing the Course and that saved Ronnie and I having to move Married Quarters to a new garrison. The staff at Tidworth Dental Centre were all very friendly and I started to settle into my new role within the Army. I worked in surgery with Major Frank Watson RADC, a Scottish workaholic. Most dentists dealt with one patient at a time but Frank had at least four on the go at any one time. He would anaesthetise a patient and put the relevant documents on the tray and send him out into the waiting room till he went numb. He would repeat this three more times so we had four dental trays and documents on the go at one time. He would then call the first guy back in and start his treatment, after making sure the patient was totally anaesthetised.

Frank treated more patients than any other dentist during Sick Parade and saw more patients during the day than Alan Sugar fired workers in an entire month. This was fine for him as he never ate anything during the day, but as he usually tried to talk some patients into continuing their treatment through the lunch-hour, it could become a problem for me as a diabetic. The single QARANC Dental Nurses came to work with a packed lunch provided by the cookhouse; they did not have time to travel to the cookhouse and eat a meal and get back for their first appointment in the afternoon. At about 1100 hours one morning my blood sugar started to drop quite rapidly as we had seen ten gazillion patients on Sick Parade as usual, Frank noticed I was more confused and inept than usual and sent me out to get something to eat to arrest my hypoglycaemic attack. He continued to treat his patients a lot more efficiently than when I was there assisting him, aspirating the water in the patient's mouth at the same time as he drilled the tooth. He also mixed the amalgam for the fillings and loaded the amalgam carriers before filling the tooth cavity. He did the lot himself.

Meanwhile, back at the ranch, I was in the restroom sweating and gibbering like a congenital idiot, and as my blood sugar dropped to a dangerous level I became more and more confused. I knew I needed to get something to eat but I hadn't bought anything in with me. I usually drove about a mile to my Married Quarter for lunch. I suddenly became aware of six white cardboard lunch boxes on the worktop. Each had a name written on it in biro: QPte Waugh, QPte Penny, QCpl Wilcox, etc. I opened the boxes and took out the cheese and pickle sandwiches and took off the cellophane wrapping, I then opened the bread and took out the cheese and pickle and made a cricket ball size bundle of smelly sticky gunge before wrapping the now empty sandwiches back up and putting them back in the lunchboxes. You are probably wondering why I did this – well, 27 years later I am still as confused as you are right now, and it doesn't get any better. I went back into the corridor where there were six doors leading into each dental surgery. I knelt down and started squeezing the cheese and pickle morass into the keyholes of each surgery like a glazier putting putty around a window. Major Frank Watson came out into the corridor looking for me and asked, "What the hell are you doing Lance Corporal Clacy?" I tutted and raised my eyebrows as it was quite obvious what I was doing, even to an ignoramus like him. "I'm putting cheese into the keyholes to stop the water coming in, what does it look like I am fucking doing?" I replied. Poor old Frank went back into his surgery scratching and shaking his head. The girls were also a bit nonplussed when they piled into their packed lunch at lunchtime.

I had another very bad hypo after being posted to Wolfenbuttel on the East-West German border about 18 months later. It was a one chair Dental Centre in Wolfenbuttel and the dentist was a balding young Irishman called Captain Keith Fullerton, who had next to no military knowledge or experience. His dental nurse was Elaine, the gorgeous wife of the muscular and handsome unit PTI Sergeant (sometimes women can be so shallow!). The three of us were there to give dental support to 2 RTR (Royal Tank Regiment) who were a London and Kent recruited unit. I ran the office of the Dental Centre and carried out some of the laboratory work but had to cover for Elaine in the surgery when she was on leave or when Captain Fullerton and I had to help out at the Dental Department of BMH Hanover for two days every fortnight. This involved staying overnight in the hospitals fleapit of a transit accommodation.

Captain Fullerton went away on a skiing Exercise and Elaine was on leave, which left me holding the fort for about two weeks. I would see all patients on Sick Parade, which included the Service families, and refer any I couldn't deal with to the Dental Officer at Dental Centre Hildeshiem, which was about an hour's drive away from Wolfenbuttel.

On this particular day the only patient who came in was a blonde-haired wife of one of the Full Screws from 2 RTR, who had the start of a nagging toothache. I had been for a run the night before and it was having a knock-on effect with my blood sugar when she came in mid-morning. I got out her documents and sat her in the dental chair in Captain Fullerton's surgery. It was an old Rathbone hydraulic chair that was elevated and lowered by pumping large pedals under the seat. By the time we got to this stage my blood sugar was dropping rapidly and I was becoming more and more confused and sweaty. I pumped the chair as high as it would go and let it drop down again. I then pulled the back of the chair into a horizontal position before pushing it back into the upright position. I then repeated this procedure for about 5 minutes until the patient became giddy and nauseous. At no stage did she question what I was doing. On examining the inside of the patient's mouth I stretched her cheeks until she looked like Krusty the Clown and put my right eye as far into her mouth as I could to try and see what the problem was. I felt I couldn't get a good view of the inside of her mouth and suggested that she lie on the floor, which she did. Again, at no stage did she question what I was doing. I told her she probably had an abscess and would need some antibiotics. After getting some Flagyl from the drugs cabinet I started throwing them at her as she lay on the floor. It wasn't the best way of getting drugs into a patient but, as I have already stated, I was very confused. Again, at no stage, etc, etc, etc...

After leaving the surgery I went into the Dental Centre office and collapsed into an armchair. The poor woman in the surgery started to question what was happening after lying on the surgery floor for another very uncomfortable 15 minutes. She went into the Pay Office next door and told the Pay Sergeant that the drunk next door needed sorting out. The pay guys knew I was a diabetic and carried me over to the Medical Centre after my distraught patient had stormed out.

I came round sitting in a wheelchair in the treatment room with the RMO administering IV glucose in my left arm and asking me what had happened over in the Dental Centre. I had some vague recollections of a blonde-haired woman and trying to get my head into her mouth like a lion tamer in a circus. I started to worry about whether or not I had assaulted her and chopped the body up and hidden it behind the sterilizer. The RMO told me not to worry about it, he would straighten the whole incident out and then he sent me off to BMH Hanover to get my blood sugars sorted out. I ended up staying in hospital for about a week.

When I came back to Wolfenbuttel I decided to find the patient I had upset and reassure her I was not the Drunken Dental Dope she thought I was. By chance I saw her in the NAAFI whilst out shopping with Ronnie on Saturday afternoon. She was down one end of an aisle and I was at the other when I recognised her and shouted, "That's her!" She saw me and a look of surprised horror registered on her face as she started running down the next aisle whilst pushing her shopping trolley full of groceries and dragging her two small children to the safety of the NAAFI Manager's office.

I made matters even worse by chasing after her with my own overflowing trolley, shouting, "Come back! I'm not mad!" I could hear her panic-ridden voice shouting, "Fuck off you alkie!" I thought she was being a bit overdramatic when she shouted, "For God's sake save the children!" When I explained to her about my diabetic condition and hypoglycaemic attacks she was very gracious and said she felt rather foolish about her outburst. Her husband called her a 'doughnut'.

I moved from Wolfenbuttel to a two-chair centre at Verden for a couple of years before I was posted to Old Park Barracks in Dover on promotion to Full Corporal. I served under several dentists at Dover but the best was a young Scotsman called Captain Mulford RADC, who decided both he and I should get more involved with the JLR RE (Royal Engineers) Unit we were supporting. The Junior Sappers were nicknamed FRED's (Future Royal Engineer Disasters) by the Permanent Staff. Our Headquarters gave Captain Mulford and me permission to go with the local unit on Exercises and Adventure Training. On one particular Adventure Training period we deployed to Sennybridge Training Camp, the Boss and I were asked to take charge of a group of about 9 Junior Sappers each and take them over Pen-Y-Fan on a map reading exercise. I had been over Pen-Y-Fan when I was in the JLR RCT at Taunton; it is the highest point in the Brecon Beacons and is always pissing down with rain and freezing cold – and that's in July, during the height of summer.

The Junior Sappers had a map and compass that they handed over to the next student when they took turns leading the squad. The instructors, namely Captain Mulford and I, had our own map and compass so we could keep a check on where the students were going and make sure they didn't get lost. The students were looking for a Trig Point, which is a small concrete block with an engraved metal plate giving the Trig Number and height. These are normally located on the highest peak of hills and are used for survey purposes. They are a good way of finding exactly where you are on a map.

Pen-Y-Fan can be a dangerous and exhausting place to get to, which is why the SAS use it for Selection and Training purposes. Captain Mulford took the whole thing rather lightheartedly and left the map reading to the Junior Sappers of his group whilst he followed at the back. The weather started to close in and the mist had reduced visibility to about ten meters when the Junior Sappers stopped and turned towards Captain Mulford and said, "We're lost Sir." Captain Mulford showed no sign of emotion and calmly said, "In the event of a war, young man, you may not have the benefit of an officer to dig you out of a tricky situation and you will have to solve your own problems." Inside his head he was thinking, 'Shit! What the fuck do I do now!' He ordered them, with as much authority as he could scrape together, to "Follow me" and headed uphill in the hope of getting into some clear weather and finding some point of reference to show where they were.

He set off at a cracking pace, with the Junior Sappers following, and after 20 minutes hard marching he bumped into the Trig point they were looking for, much to his great surprise. "Right, we are now at the Trig Point you were looking for," he bluffed. "This is the last time I will be digging you out of the shit. Make sure from this point onwards you know exactly where you are at all times!"

At the end of the day's training I was in the NAAFI and overheard one of the young lads in Captain Mulford's squad talking.

"That dentist is fucking brilliant at map reading," he said.

I was posted to Dental Centre Borden a couple of years later and promoted to Sergeant. The Dental Centre had two dentists and a hygienist. There was a lot more work involved in running a multi-chair centre. My Group Headquarters sent me on a Blood Transfusion Assistants Course as the RADC had to cover a new War Role within the British Army. In the event of going to war the RAMC and RADC would set up and run Blood Transfusion Centres to take blood from soldiers to build up the stock in its blood banks. The Course was about two weeks long and held in Aldershot at the Army Blood Bank near St Omer Barracks in Aldershot.

On the Course I met Sergeant Ritchie John, who was the first person since Chris Lovett who I wanted to emulate. Ritchie's dad was originally from Grenada and his mum was from Ireland. He was born and raised around Southall in West London with his older brother. He was a fitness fanatic and every day he used to visit a gymnasium after finishing work or go for a 10-mile run just for a bit of fun. He was physically very strong and had he joined the Royal Marines or Parachute Regiment I am sure he would have had the determination and single mindedness to pass the physical selection. I am not sure though if, like me, he would have been mentally aggressive enough to have wanted to follow that sort of Military life. It still puzzles me, even today, that he went into the Army Careers Office and decided to become a Tooth Fairy. At least his brother went into something more macho like the RAMC, even if it was only as a Drain Sniffer (Environmental Health Technician).

Ritchie was also the scruffiest bastard I have met in my entire military career, and that includes both in uniform and civilian attire, but he didn't give a shit about the Army etiquette of ironing a shirt and polishing his boots. I have to admit whilst my choice of civilian clothes was questionable, at least I was smart in uniform. When a senior rank in the British Army puts on their Mess Kit for a Dinner Night you cannot fail to look smart, Ritchie could and did. He used to take his clean Mess Kit golf ball shirt off the radiator and put it straight on, I have never seen him in mess kit with a straight dickie bow, and I always expected his to either start flashing and spinning or squirting water. We are talking about a man who had no interest in anything to do with the RADC, especially if it involved him doing any work. He was only interested in drinking alcohol, hard physical training and having sex with as many good looking women he could get his hands on – and as he was socially very popular he didn't have to try very hard to score.

Apart from the hard physical training you can now see why he was my hero. Ritchie was working at Dental Centre Pirbright when I met him on the BTA Course and he was always in the crap with the Lt Col he worked for, this was because he was often drunk when he bothered to turn up late for work. Ritchie spent so much time in his OC's office getting balled out for one misdemeanour or another, he decided to shag his latest female conquest on his boss's desk one night so that whilst receiving future reprimands he would have some pleasant memories whilst he wasn't listening.

During the Course we all had to go out on a blood donor session at Windsor Barracks where the Life Guards (Donkey Wallopers) were based at the time. The idea was to collect blood from soldiers for the Army Blood Banks and to give the students some experience at carrying out one of their war roles. We departed Aldershot for the hour's journey at 0700 hours on an old and uncomfortable 39-seater army bus. On the bus with us were about a dozen civilian middle-aged women who were employed by the Army as experienced BTA's who were going to teach and guide us through the practical side of the day's bloodletting. These women had been doing this job for the last 139 years of their lives and were set in their ways.

All Military Course members were on the coach when the civilian ladies arrived. Ritchie was near the front of the coach and was unfortunately sitting in seat number 7. The first lady got on the bus and when she saw where Ritchie was sitting she looked at him and tutted. The lady behind her also spotted where Ritchie had plonked his arse and said, "Oh no, this will not do!" Both of these ladies sat in the seats behind Ritchie and he heard one whisper to the other, "that's Margaret's seat. What the hell is *he* doing sitting there? There'll be ructions today, you mark my word." From the back of the bus I could see Ritchie looking about nervously and wondering what the hell he should do. He bottled it and came further up the bus and sat down. We all agreed this was a wise decision when 16 stone of Margaret marched onto the bus and started ordering people about. These ladies had sat in their own particular designated seats for years and were likely to break the spine of any unsuspecting soldier who, either bravely or in Ritchie's case ignorantly, decided to trespass on one of them.

On arrival at the Life Guards Barracks we set up the stretcher beds and all the other equipment in the gymnasium where we were going to do the blood collecting session that day. All the Course students had to wear long, white doctor's coats over our uniforms just in case there were any accidents with the blood handling, no one could therefore tell what rank we were, as we all looked like doctors. We started pissing about and calling each other in a posh manner and saying things like, "I say Doctor Adams, would you mind awfully giving me your diagnosis on this patient?" I unfortunately did this as one of the Life Guards SSMs marched up behind me and banged his heavily bulled boots together when he halted in a very smart and soldier like fashion. His large gnarled head and face was on top of a sturdy muscular body. As I turned round he threw me the sharpest salute I have ever seen in my life, peered out from under the slashed peak of his forage cap and shouted, "GOOD MORNING SAH! I'VE COME TO DONATE SOME BLOOD FOR THE GOOD AND BENEFIT OF THE BRITISH ARMY!"

There were only two ways I could deal with this situation and I didn't fancy either of them very much. I could be honest and say, "Sorry sir, I am just a Sergeant in the RADC and you have just made a monumental arse of yourself in front of everybody," which would embarrass and anger him with the likely knock-on effect of him wanting to rip my head off my shoulders. I therefore decided to save his dignity and my neck with a very risky plan of action. I put on my best Jeeves and Wooster accent and said, "Well done Sergeant Major, good to have you on board and leading by example. Be a good chap, roll up your sleeves and let me have a quick peek at your veins would you?" He rolled up his sleeves and I started prodding his arms and said, "I say! These look awfully good, well done, even the Royal Artillery could hit them, what what." He seemed very pleased with himself and went to lie on one of the beds I directed him to, which was being supervised by my old mate from Tidworth, Corporal Mark Adams RADC. I winked at Mark and said "Corporal Adams. Would you be so good and take care of my good friend the Sergeant Major here and make sure he comes to no harm." Mark smiled and said, "Leave him with me Sir, I'll take good care of him for you." I was glad I didn't run into him during our lunch break without my white coat on.

On completion of the Course we all returned to our units and I kept in touch with Ritchie over the next 18 months. He phoned one day and told me he had been given a Posting Order sending him to Dental Centre Hameln in West Germany in the next six weeks. My disappointment at him being posted was short-lived, I got a phone call from our Group Headquarters informing me I was also being posted to the same Dental Group as Ritchie, at the same time. I was going to the Dental Centre at Detmold, about 40 minutes drive away from Hameln. Ritchie became a regular fixture at my flat during the weekends when he wasn't out on the town flirting with the local fräuleins.

At our new Group Headquarters in Herford was the most efficient and dynamic Admin Clerk the world has ever been blessed with. Sergeant John King was another TFI from the DERR (Duke of Edinburgh Royal Regiment) and was a very good friend of Jeff Bush, who was on my DCA 3 Course. He was a very good footballer and had played at either Corps or Army level. You have to be very fit and dedicated to play at that level. He had a face that can only be described as a screaming skull and yet, as ugly as he was, women were attracted to him like bears to a honeypot because he was so charismatic. As an ex Infantryman he was also tough as old boots and had the quickest wit of any man I have ever met. I would hold anyone in high esteem if they had the guts to heckle or take him on in a one-to-one fight.

I believe John could and should have gone on to be the Corps RSM but for the sake of his married and family life he decided to leave the army and give up drinking alcohol completely as, and I quote from him, "I am a Right Royal Pain in the Arse when I am pissed." It was the Corps and Army's loss the day he decided to PVR (Pre Voluntary Release).

No-one at Group Headquarters seemed to be bothered that John was leaving and although the Sergeants Mess would dine him out, Ritchie and I felt something more personal and friendly should be done to see him off into Civvy Street. Ritchie and I arranged to meet John in the Sergeants Mess at Herford with Ritchie's Dental Officer 'Buster Gonad'. Buster was like no Dental Officer I have ever met in my life; he would have been better placed as a Private in the ACC (Army Catering Corps). He and Ritchie were more like best mates than the usual Officer and SNCO relationship. The four of us had a few pints in the Mess before heading to downtown Herford for a night on the piss. John told us he was on the wagon and did not have a drop of alcohol all night, in fact he drove his car to ferry us around. No amount of persuasion could get him to have a pint. As we had met up in the Sergeants Mess bar we had to wear jackets and ties, so we continued on our farewell mission in the nightlife of Herford in the same smart attire. Well, me, John and Buster were smart, Ritchie did the best he could. We looked so out of place among the other soldiers on the piss in Herford who were all wearing casual clothing. By the time we ended up at a nightclub called 'The Ice Rink' three of us in our group were pissed out of our tiny minds. The Ice Rink was a massive club with several different stages that live bands performed on; it was very noisy with about four different bands playing at the same time. There were several bars scattered about the place and some very large and muscled doormen, who wouldn't have looked out of place in the Kray gang, patrolling each bar and dance area.

Buster was on the dance floor trying to do some break dancing; he looked more like he was doing a very good impression of a dying cockroach. Some of the local fräuleins were also getting very annoyed as they fell over his prostrate body and ending up in an undignified heap on the floor. The three of us were pissing ourselves with laughter at him when the 'doormen' moved in. John apologised to them and said he would make sure we would not cause any more problems if they agreed not to throw us out. Reluctantly they agreed, as John was obviously sober and sensible they took him at his word. Big mistake. I noticed on one of the stages a German oompah band who were wearing mountain hats and *lederhosen* – the traditional Bavarian leather shorts with braces. They were all sitting down facing the dance floor, playing a mixture of brass instruments. Buster and I decided to join them on stage and pretended to be playing a couple of trombones. The audience seemed to find this very funny, in particular the Royal Signals soldiers from the resident local unit. The 'doormen' took a different view, however, and seemed somewhat annoyed. From our viewpoint on the stage Buster and I could see them coming. He nudged me and said "Run for it Harry, the Goons are coming!" We moved between the two back rows of musicians and shuffled towards the other side of the stage, saying, "Excuse me ... sorry about this ... would you mind awfully if I squeezed through."

Instead of sensibly waiting for us to come off the stage, the Goons chased us between the rows of musicians. Once at the other side of the stage we doubled back between the first and second rows of bona fide trombone players. The Goons made a grab for us and we sent three musicians flying onto the dance floor. Not surprisingly, the music seemed to take on a less professional sound. All four of us were frog marched out of the nightclub and told never to darken their doorstep again. John dragged Buster away as he was shouting "Come on, we can take the bastards!"

What a fantastic night it was! Even John, who was as sober as a judge, thoroughly enjoyed watching the three of us making total arses of ourselves.

John left the Army and went to work for his father-in-law on his caravan site in the West Country.

14. D MED

My boss at Dental Centre Detmold was a great guy called Major Pretsall RADC who was a good dentist as well as an extremely efficient administrator, he was also a hard task-master who expected nothing more from his staff than he would do himself. I would have pitted the Garrison's dental fitness states at Detmold against any other unit in the British Army. During the two and a half years we worked together I learned so much about army administration from him; he also taught me not to jump from one job to another without completing your current task.

When Major Pretsall was posted, his replacement was Colonel Lampard RADC, who actually outranked the Group Headquarters CO, who was only a Lt-Colonel. Colonel Lampard was getting near his retirement age and had no interest in Dental Fitness States or doing much of any work at all. Consequently our percentage of dentally fit soldiers in the Garrison dropped from about 87% down to about 49% and I started getting phone calls from the Group Headquarters Admin Officer Lieutenant Dick. "Your Dental Fitness States are dropping to an unacceptable level. Start getting soldiers in for dental inspections and treatment or there will be serious trouble for you Sergeant Clacy. Start doing your job properly!" After informing Colonel Lampard of what I had been told he stated in a blasé manner, "This is my Dental Centre and I will not be dictated to by anyone at Group Headquarters, now get out of my office!"

I was like an umpire at a verbal tennis match between Group and my boss and neither side actually wanted to speak to the other. I eventually reported up at Group Headquarters and had an interview with Lieutenant Dick to explain about Colonel Lampard's aversion to work. He told me that he and the CO would soon have this sorted out when they came down to Detmold on an official visit, he thanked me for being so diplomatic and for trying to sort out the matter with the Colonel. I eagerly awaited the official visit as the whole petty matter was getting on my tits and as it was coming round to Confidential Report time I didn't want to get a bad report resulting in a non recommendation for promotion to Staff Sergeant.

When the CO visited he walked into the Colonel's office and said, "Hello Mike! How wonderful to see you, it's been a few years. How is your lovely wife?"

'Yeah, go on sir,' I thought. 'Butter him up before you verbally stick it straight on his chin.'

Lieutenant Dick and the CO were only in the office for about twenty minutes before they came out with Colonel Lampard saying, "It's been super to see you again Stuart, we must arrange to have dinner one night with our wives."

They both left the Dental Centre and returned to Group Headquarters without saying a word to me or any other member of staff. Colonel Lampard was equally silent and I was more than a little confused. Everything carried on in the same vein as before. My good friend Sergeant John King, the efficient and dynamic Admin Clerk at Group Headquarters, gave me a copy of a confidential letter from Group Headquarters to the Dental Brigadier at Dusseldorf. I had been hung out to dry and made a scapegoat for Colonel Lampard. The letter had been composed and signed by Lieutenant Dick and it stated that 'Sergeant Clacy was out of his depth at Dental Centre Detmold and they would review my future placement with great care'. John King would have got into a lot of trouble about giving me a copy of the letter but he knew what was happening at Detmold and felt morally obliged to put me in the picture. I waited until his PVR had gone through before taking it up to Lieutenant Dick and demanding an explanation. He went absolutely ballistic and demanded to know how I got a copy of the letter. When I told him the letter was sent to me anonymously he started shouting, "Get out of my office, get back to your Dental Centre and stop snooping into things that don't concern you!" What a berk. How could it not concern me when the whole letter was *about* me?

When the Brigadier eventually came to visit our Dental Centre with his WO 2 clerk, I explained what had happened since Major Pretsall had left and asked for his advice as an experienced Warrant Officer within the RADC. He said, and I quote, "I hate you fucking TFI's, you come into my Corps from other units and think you are the bees fucking knees, well you ain't. If I had to make a choice for a promotion selection between a direct entrant who was a complete wanker and you, even if you were good at your job, I would give it to the direct entrant every time! Don't bother me with your trivial little problems." Nice guy.

I decided to take matters into my own hands and arranged to take a posting to DMed (Defence Medical Equipment Depot) in Bielefeld to replace an RADC Sergeant who was getting promoted to Staff Sergeant. A Corporal from Lemgo was promoted to Sergeant to replace me at Detmold, poor bastard. Manning and Records and Group Headquarters agreed the posting swap and I headed off to Bielefeld, where I had started in the army at 10 Regiment. DMed was co-located at Richmond Barracks with 6 Ordnance Battalion RAOC.

At secret locations around BAOR, complete medical equipment holdings for units based in the UK were stored ready for use. If the Russians came across the border looking for a fight, UK units would collect their equipment from these secret locations and deploy straight into the field ready for military operations. The Military personnel at DMed were tasked to go around these locations, collect all the kit and bring it back to Bielefeld, overhaul its contents and then return it ready for use when required. Each set of holdings was overhauled every two years on a rotation system. My job at DMed was to check all the mobile dental equipment that was held within each equipment scale. It was an easy job and I was out of the RADC system for a while and back with a proper working unit.

In DMed there were a couple of REME technicians who serviced all electrical equipment in the unit kit we overhauled and a lot of civilian workers. Apart from us, everyone else in the Depot were RAMC Medical storemen. The unit had about three officers, who included an OC with the rank of Major, a

WO1 RSM, about six SNCOs, ten JNCOs and two privates. The rank structure did seem a bit top-heavy, Pte Rolfie Halstead RAMC, who came from Clitheroe in West Yorkshire, once asked me, "Eh up Sarge, wi so many wankas int DMed, ahr cum ahm stuk at fuckin bottom?" Every soldier feels that way at some stage in his career and it can be very frustrating, however the majority of the staff at DMed were excellent young men with quick wits and dirty minds.

I had settled into the day-to-day routine of 'turning over' the dental kits withdrawn into DMed when Saddam Hussein and his armies invaded Kuwait. Behind the scenes the media and Joe Public saw, the British Armed Forces went into hyperdrive in preparation for going to war again. This time I would be more involved, I would be assembling kit for field ambulances and hospitals ready for their deployment into the desert in Saudi Arabia. Some of the kit required by medical units was not available and we had to visit the secret locations around BAOR and temporarily rob them of the required items. The whole unit, including civilians, worked literally around the clock to get everything ready for units deploying on Operation 'Granby'.

I had not worked so long and hard since leaving the RCT but I loved the community spirit that bound us all together in our aim to help prepare the British Army Medical Services for war. DMed as a unit also deployed to the Gulf but in a formation called 84 F Med (Field Medical Equipment Depot) and it would resupply and replace any medical items required, including drugs, to every medical unit deployed in the area of operations. A select few were told they were going to deploy and were overjoyed at the prospect of going to war. They were no different to the young lads of 1914 who wanted to prove their mettle. This was the second war in my time in the army and frustratingly, again, I was not going. However, I was going to be involved indirectly.

My son Matthew was, by this time, a qualified chef serving with 20 Squadron RAF Regiment, a Rapier Anti-Aircraft Missile unit. His unit was one of the first to start deploying out to the Middle East. Matt phoned us at home from Cyprus to let us know he was nervous but we were not to worry as he had a lot of good tough mates who would look after him. As a father I felt useless for the first time in the 14 years of his life that I had been his dad. He was going to war and there was nothing I could do to help or protect him, I thought 'why the fuck have they sent him out there and not me?' We didn't have a lot of time to talk, as other servicemen needed to use the phones to contact their families. I remembered how I felt after Chris had left to fight in the Falklands War and I told Matthew how proud I was of him and that I loved him very much. Ronnie, Naomi, Daniel and I all wept as a family.

During the build up to the war it seemed most units from BAOR and the UK were involved one way or another and the MOD was worried about the Chemical Capability of Saddam's Armies. So were DMed and they tasked me with training the young lads deploying from our unit to improve their NBC skills. For years NBC instructors like myself had tried to teach about a subject no-one was interested in – after all, there was no way the Russians were going to invade West Germany, and if they did there was no way they would dare use chemical weapons. All of a sudden officers who had been too busy playing golf at Sennelager to attend my lectures grabbed me and said, "Sergeant Clacy, they are sending me out to the Gulf. For fuck's sake teach me everything you know about NBC. I am flying out there in the next two hours!"

I put the lads from the unit through their paces on the football pitch at Catterick Barracks and made them carry out urination and defecation drills for real. With hindsight, as the entrance to the families NAAFI was just the other side of a wire fence, it might have been prudent to have put a tent up to carry out these drills. Having said that, Smurf, Biggy and Frankie Short all seemed to enjoy the feel of a warm summer breeze on their bare arses as they crouched down and I walked up and down, making sure they did everything properly. The young lads threw themselves into the training with such gusto and enthusiasm that I felt proud to be their instructor.

Things seemed to slow down a bit once units had started to fly and sail out to the Gulf and I found the routine boring after all the hype and urgency of the previous month or so. As well as the Iraqi NBC Threat, the MOD Chief of Staff was also concerned about how many casualties the Coalition Forces would suffer, especially if the Iraqi's used chemical weapons. They arranged for a massive training centre to be organised at Sennelager to train the next wave of troops deploying. There would be training in NBC, First Aid, Skill at Arms, the Laws of Armed Conflict and a host of other subjects. The Training Centre was called BCR (Battle Casualty Replacements) Headquarters but once the media got wind of the name it was dropped because of the word casualty, the media got a lot of mileage out the fact that soldiers could possibly get killed or maimed. The media, in all wars, are like circling vultures waiting for the bodies to be piled up and they can fight over getting the best pictures of the suffering and dead. There's no news like bad news.

An order was disseminated for all units in BAOR to send their instructors to 15/19 KRH (Kings Royal Hussars) who were the unit tasked with organising and arranging the whole BCR Headquarters set up. DMed sent me as their contribution towards the war effort as I could instruct in First Aid and NBC, but as I had considerable experience in casualty simulation I was incorporated in the First Aid instructing complex. The people that were going to organise this massive training complex were given a budget so big they could have started their own private war. As a SNCO from DMed I was sent back there with two 4 Tonners to collect as many shell dressings, bandages, IV fluids and as much casualty simulation kit as it was possible to cram on board. Each complex had more kit to train with than the entire British Army had used over the preceding five years. Audiovisual equipment appeared in every classroom and they were virtually throwing kit at us. No expense was spared.

Most of the instructors in the First Aid complex were RAMC CMTs (Combat Medical Technicians) from 4 ADFA (Armoured Field Ambulance); they were energetic and very enthusiastic in every part of the training syllabus. They even made mock ups of helicopters to simulate evacuating casualties in different types of choppers. They also got hold of some children's rubber dolls and made them up with wounds and had soldiers running around with tea towels on their heads pretending to be Arab civilian casualties. It was to make the soldiers learn about treating casualties by triage and not just selecting British casualties first. We also taught everyone to strip British casualties of water, food, ammunition and any other kit that may be of use after the casualties have been evacuated. A casualty should be sent back with only his uniform, respirator and personal weapon, the trainees seemed delighted when we told them that within an hour of being injured he would be back in a Field Hospital getting a blow-job from an army nurse. Those left behind cannot be sure when they are likely to get their next re-supply and would have to make good use of anything that was available.

The instructors worked from 0500 hours through to 2300 hours daily preparing for lessons, clearing up after the days training, actually instructing on the lessons and attending briefings by the BCR Headquarters staff. It was probably the hardest I have worked in my life and that would probably include serving in Northern Ireland. The paradox of the whole situation was that I never suffered from any hypoglycaemic attacks during the months that I worked at Sennelager Training Camp.

Some of the classes we were instructing too could be as large as fifty soldiers. They usually dragged themselves into the stables where we held the lessons looking very tired and totally pissed off. It was going to be mission impossible to get these 'fucked about' soldiers interested in yet another military-style lecture. I got hold of some very hard core pornography on videos and started running it on the audio-visual monitor as soon as they trudged in. They quickly threw off their webbing and scrambled to get a front seat view. I let it run for about three minutes and then switched it off to the sounds of "Hey! We were watching that! Can't you leave it on!" I told them they were with me for a forty-minute lecture on Intravenous Infusions and if they paid attention and answered my questions correctly I would put the video back on for the last five minutes of their lesson with me. It worked every time. I personally thought that of every lesson the troops learned during this period, setting up a drip on a casualty was the most important.

At the end of the day's training all the instructors met in the Sergeants Mess to watch the Sky News TV reports on the Air War taking place over Iraq and all the preparations in Saudi Arabia to get the Ground Forces ready for the liberation of Kuwait. I bumped into Ritchie John in the bar one night, drinking with other SNCOs from 3 ADFA.

"What the fuck are you doing here" I enquired.

This is his sorry tale.

Ritchie had decided to try his luck on a commissioning board to become an officer in the British Army. He wasn't selected and was advised to try again the following year as he had "almost come up to the mark" on that particular Board. They probably assessed him as being too intelligent and smart to become a British Army Officer. You can't become an officer in the British Army if you have been circumcised – you have to be a complete prick. The board tried to persuade Ritchie to go on what RMA Sandhurst refer to as a 'Knife and Fork Course' to improve his social manners. Whilst scratching his arse he said "Nah! You can fuck that for a game of soldiers!" He then went back to his unit and signed off. This meant he would be out of the Army within twelve months.

This had happened about eight months previously and he was happily tossing off his last four months in the Army at Dental Centre Osnabruck when his OC came and had a little chat. His OC had asked Ritchie about one month earlier to organise a lunchtime conference at the Dental Centre conference room for about a dozen high-ranking officers, which included the RADC's Brigadier. Ritchie informed his OC that he had about four months to serve and had no intention of doing anything for anyone, especially any officers. The OC ordered Ritchie to organise the conference or there would be trouble and he must include a small buffet lunch and drinks. Ritchie would, of course, have to walk round, topping up wine glasses as they were quaffed.

Anyone who knows Ritchie John would automatically realise that he was going to dig his heels in and not do a damn thing, and that is exactly what happened. Every time the OC asked Ritchie how the preparations were progressing he would say, "Yep! Don't worry Sir, it will be alright on the night." Come the day of the conference the OC was perplexed, as nothing seemed to be happening. With about an hour to go before the guests started arriving.

"Sergeant John! Sergeant John! What is happening with the conference? What have you organised?"

"I told you sir," Ritchie replied. "I have about four months to serve and I have no interest in you, your conference or anything else to do with the British Army. I don't care what happens to you or your conference and there is nothing you can do to me as I will be leaving the Army soon."

The conference was a disaster and there was very little the OC could do to Ritchie. It was at this time that the OC called Ritchie into his office for his little chat.

"Ah, Sergeant John, I've been asked if I will release you for attachment to 3 ADFA to bring them up to scale of personnel required for deployment out to the Gulf War. I really can't think of one good reason why I shouldn't agree to this attachment, can you?"

"Yes I fucking well can," Ritchie said. "I've only got sixteen weeks to go before I'm out of the Army. You can't possibly send me."

"Oh yes I can," the OC quietly replied.

And that was how Ritchie's sorry arse ended up at Sennelager, training to get ready for war and complaining to anyone who would listen.

"Sixteen fucking weeks to go in the army, sixteen fucking weeks and I'm going to die in a cloud of fucking nerve agent!"

Still, it was good that we could all laugh about it.

After the war was over and DMed returned to the normal routine I listened to a hundred and one hilarious stories from young lads who had served in what was their first and hopefully last armed conflict. One of these young lads was a very young Full Screw called Frankie Short, who was an archetypal cockney wide-boy. He was a very fit NCO and wore thick glasses that couldn't hide a wicked glint in his eyes. He made Del-boy from Only Fools and Horses sound like an Oxford Don. The unit had a function to welcome them all back,

Frankie had spoken to the OC months previously, prior to going off to the Gulf…

OC: "Hello Corporal Short, how are you?"

Frankie: "Fine fank you sir."

OC: "Are you looking forward to going out to Saudi Arabia?"

Frankie: "Not if I'm gonna get killed sir."

(Not listening to Frankie's reply he continued)

OC: "How is your wife settling in over here in Germany?"

Frankie: "I ain't married sir."

OC: "Oh! Are you sure? I could have sworn you were married."

(Frankie looks around slightly confused)

Frankie: "I fink I would know if I 'ad an old Duchess at 'ome sir."

❖ ❖ ❖

Just before leaving for the Gulf the OC had another little chat with the lads…

OC: "Hello Corporal Short, how are you?"

Frankie: "Fine fank you sir, looking forward to gettin arht there and doin' the business."

OC: "Good man, well done, and how is your wife coping with it all?"

Frankie: "I've told you before sir, I ain't married."

OC: "Oh.. really? But I was sure you were. Oh, never mind."

Frankie: (mutters under his breath) "For fuck's sake you dozy old bastard."

❖ ❖ ❖

At the welcome back function poor old Frankie was again collared by the OC for another informal friendly talk…

OC: "Ah, Corporal Short, good to see you back safe and well."

Frankie: "Fank you sir, its bleedin great to get a couple of cold ones dahn the old Gregory Peck."

OC: "I'm sure your wife must be pleased to see you back safe and sound."

Frankie: Oh my giddy aunt … Yeah she's dead chuffed sir … especially as we're avin a baby soon. We're goin' to call him Neville after you sir."

OC: "Well done, congratulations Corporal Short … RSM Crisp? Did you know Corporal Short and his wife were going to have a baby?"

The RSM looked sternly at Frankie.

"No sir I didn't… Corporal Short, you must pop up to my office later and tell me all about it."

❖ ❖ ❖

The Government were probably very disappointed that more soldiers didn't die out in the battle for Kuwait, because they had to pay out and make them all redundant when they came back alive. I was one of those soldiers selected for redundancy and saw Ritchie go off to Civvy Street about six months prior to me. Before leaving Germany I attended an address given by a Full Colonel in the Garrison cinema in Ripon Barracks. All soldiers being made redundant had to attend the briefing so we would understand what was going to happen to us in the final stages of our Army careers. On looking around the full cinema I saw a wealth of hard-bitten and experienced soldiers, from privates all the way up to a couple of brigadiers.

It was sad that the Army was going to throw out these tough and loyal servants of the Crown because they now deemed us surplus to requirements.

Epilogue

Shortly before leaving the army on redundancy I was Orderly Sergeant at Richmond Barracks for my last official duty in the Regular British Army. I was 36 years old. The Orderly Officer was a Warrant Officer Class 2 from the Royal Army Ordnance Corps (Blanket Stackers). He listened as I told him of my trepidation at leaving the Army and my disappointment at not progressing further up the rank structure in my military career. I explained about the farce with Colonel Lampard and Lieutenant Dick and that I felt it was their shortcomings that ultimately led to my failure in gaining promotion, even though I had more courses and qualifications under my belt than most Warrant Officers. I was taken aback when he quietly and calmly told me that the failure to gain promotion was mine and mine alone. Somewhat put out, I asked him to explain how he came to such a ridiculous conclusion.

"Officers in the British Army want answers not questions, they want solutions not problems. You made them ask questions and face up to a problem and the answer to the problem was to get rid of you."

I was totally confused, so I asked him how he would have solved the problem of the falling dental fitness states and the badgering phone calls I was getting from Group HQ.

He told me what his three-point plan would have been if he were in my position:

1. Let Colonel Lampard finish his time in the army in any fashion he wanted and whatever he asked me to do, my reply should always have been "Yes Sir!"

2. When doing the dental monthly returns to Group Headquarters I should have falsified the figures and made them look as good as Group Headquarters wanted them to be.

3. Whenever contacted by Group Headquarters my reply, whatever the question, should always be "Yes Sir!"

"What about the dental fitness of the soldiers in Detmold Garrison?" I asked. "It would be unfair on them."

"Fuck 'em," he replied. "That wasn't your problem if you wanted to get promoted."

I didn't agree with him and said at least my integrity was intact, to which he replied, "Yeah! That's great, but I'm nine years younger than you and yet two ranks higher. You can keep your fucking integrity."

He was probably right, and anyway I felt at the time that I was ready to move out into civilian life – and a £56,000 redundancy package and pension was certainly going to help. It was a good deal because I had served 18 years 180 days and it was more than I would have received had I completed the full 22 years.

I served my last six months in the Army as an NBC and First Aid instructor at 250 Field Ambulance RAMC in Wenlock Barracks, Hull. When I initially arrived at the unit WO1 RSM (Later Captain) Donny Stewart RAMC interviewed me and asked if I intended to 'stick my thumb up my arse for the next six months' or get involved in the unit exercises and social life. He said the unit could definitely put my skills and enthusiasm to good use but if I wanted to see out my time left in the Army 'tossing it off' he would understand and I could de-kit now and go home. I decided to stay and see what the unit was like; after all, they were just a bunch of Northern STABs (Stupid Territorial Army Bastards). I was slightly worried about the reputation of 'Northerners' as being a tough, punchy lot from mining and trawling stock. Some of the lads in the Regular British Army I had met were definitely of that ilk. Donny assured me that they were a great bunch and were enthusiastic soldiers, but also liked to party as much as possible.

The first TA Medic I met from the unit was Private Debbie Tuff. She had an attractive face, short blonde hair and the finest pair of breasts on any soldier I had met in the Regular and Territorial Army. Her first East Yorkshire words to me were "Who the fuck are you Sarge?"

I explained my situation and said, "I'm going to try and make decent soldiers out of you thick Northerners."

She gave me a beautiful grin and said, "Oh no! Not another RASH (Regular Army Shit Head) in the unit!"

The unit was full of characters like her and included Pte Adam Broom, who had obviously joined the TA to see as much action as he could, although most of the action he saw was on the unit pool table and in the back of the TA ambulances with female TA Medics. He also did a tough tour of duty in the early days of the troubles in Bosnia. He had a thirst for Combat Medicine and Casualty Simulation that seemed insatiable. Fifteen years later he is a Paramedic working on the Three Shires Helicopter Air Ambulance and is one of my closest friends.

One of the first Exercises I did with 250 Field Ambulance was a TA Annual Camp in Browndown Camp in Portsmouth. The RSM, WO 1 Donny Stewart, was very impressed with my Casualty Simulation skills. Three years later he arranged for me to fly out to Northern Ireland and do most of the Casualty Simulation for the NIFAC (Northern Ireland First Aid Competition) and the following year fly out a team of eight TA Cassimers, who I had trained in 250 Field Ambulance, for the same annual competition. Donny Stewart was instrumental in persuading me to join 250 Field Ambulance as a TA soldier after I had been discharged from the Regular Army. I spent five years in the TA and enjoyed it immensely. I discovered that the 'fucking thick Northerners' weren't thick, but the friendliest, most inquisitive and some of the funniest people I have had the pleasure to meet and serve with.

I also got a job as a Civil Servant, working at Imphal Barracks in York, and have subsequently moved to the Defence School of Transport at Leconfield, doing the same job.

I had been married to Ronnie for twenty years and felt I could not stand her negative attitudes any longer. I walked into a solicitor's office in Hull and implemented divorce proceedings on the grounds of unreasonable behaviour. It took a lot of courage (certainly more than I displayed as a soldier) to start this. I just felt I couldn't face another twenty years of constantly having to reassure and mentally support someone else. I moved into a surplus Married Quarter in York and when my Decree Absolute came through in the post I felt like a giant black cloud had been moved away.

Matt was still serving in the RAF, Naomi was married to a soldier serving in BAOR and Daniel was training to become a chef at college in Bridlington. They all had difficulty in coming to terms with the fact that I had divorced their mother and I lost contact with Daniel for about ten years. We are now reconciled and I often visit him and his wife at their house in Bridlington. Naomi has written to me and explained that she understands why I divorced her mum but out of loyalty to her she feels she cannot meet me. Matt has constantly been in contact with me and after leaving the RAF he joined my old TA (Territorial Army) unit at 250 Field Ambulance in Hull. He also deployed on the second Gulf War but this time as a TA CMT (Combat Medical Technician). He has openly admitted that it was much more difficult than his first deployment with the RAF and has been under treatment for PTSD (Post Traumatic Stress Disorder).

Last year at Bowness-on-Windermere in the Lake District I married my beautiful wife Nicky, who is so out of my league. I feel about ten feet tall when I walk down the street holding her hand.

For the first time in my life, I don't feel like a Crap Hat.

~ End ~

Glossary

ABA..........................Amateur Boxing Association
APTC........................Army Physical Training Corps
Bedford RL.............3 TON Heavy Goods Vehicle
Bluebell ....Code name on military radio network for REME
BMH ....British Military Hospital
Bürgermeister........Mayor of German Town
Coffee Pot...............Code name on military radio network for WRAC personnel
Compo Rations......Tinned and dry rations in a box for field conditions
CP ....Command Post
Cpl ....Corporal (Two Stripes)
Crap Hat.................Any soldier not serving in Airborne Forces
DMed ....Defence Medical Equipment Depot
DMS ....British Army (Directly Moulded Soles) ankle boots
DPM ....Disruptive Pattern Material (Camouflage Material)
Diggers ....Knife Fork and Spoon
Flak Jacket..............US designed sleeveless protective vest
Full Screw...............Corporal
Gastatte ....German Restaurant/Bar
G1098 ....General admin stores in barracks and on Exercise
HGV.........................heavy Goods Vehicle
IED ....Improvised Explosive Devise
IRA...........................Irish Republican Army
J/Dvr........................Junior Driver (Lowest rank in the JLR RCT)
JLR ....Junior Leaders Regiment
LCpl ....Lance Corporal (Commonly referred to as Lance Jack - One Stripe)
LI..............................Light Infantry
LTA...........................Load Transfer Area
MCTC ....Military Correction Training Centre (Military Prison Colchester)
MFO ....Military Freight Organisation
M K ....4-Ton Heavy Goods Vehicle

MPSC........................Military Provost Staff Corps (Military Prison Wardens)
NAAFI......................Navy Army Air Force Institute (Forces Shopping Complex)
Napalm ....Petroleum Jelly Bomb that explodes on contact with ground
NATO.......................North Atlantic Treaty Organization
NBC.........................Nuclear Biological and Chemical
NCO.........................Non-Commissioned Officer (Lance Corporal to WO1)
NI.............................Northern Ireland
NITTAT...................Northern Ireland Tactics and Training Team
OC...........................Officer Commanding (Sqn or Coy commander of Major rank)
Para..........................Paratrooper
Playtime.................Code Name on Radio for any RCT Personnel
PTI ....Physical Training Instructor (Commonly Referred to as Meatballs)
QLR..........................Queens Lancashire Regiment (Infantry)
QMSI ....Quarter Master Staff Instructor (WO2 in charge of all PTIs)
QM's ....Quarter Master Stores
RADC......................Royal Army Dental Corps
RAF..........................Royal Air Force
RAMC ....Royal Army Medical Corps
RAOC......................Royal Army Ordnance Corps
RCT.........................Royal Corps of Transport
Regt ....Regiment
REME ....Royal Electrical and Mechanical Engineers
RGJ...........................Royal Green Jackets (Infantry)
RHQ........................Regimental Headquarters
RMP........................Royal Military Police (Commonly referred to as Monkeys)
RQMS ....Regimental Quarter Master Sergeant (WO2)
RSM........................Regimental Sergeant Major (WO1)
SAS..........................Special Air Services
Sgt...........................Sergeant (Three Stripes)
SIB ....Special Investigation Branch (Detectives of the RMPs)
Skiddies..................Underpants
SLR ....7.62mm Self-Loading Rifle
SMG........................9mm Sub Machine Gun

SSgt..........................Staff Sergeant (Three Stripes with a Crown above it)
SSM ....Squadron Sergeant Major (WO2)
SQMS.......................Squadron Quarter Master Sergeant (SSgt)
Sqn ....Squadron
TTF ....Transporter Tanker Fuel (22,000 Litre and 12,500 Litre)
VCP..........................Vehicle Check Point
VM ....Vehicle Mechanic (REME)
WO1.........................Warrant Officer Class 1 (Lion and Unicorn Crest worn on right forearm)
WO2.........................Warrant Officer Class 2 (Crown worn on right forearm)
WRAC ....Women's Royal Army Corps
WRVS.......................Women's Royal Volunteer Service (Recreational Club)